Helping Children
with Problems

Helping Children With Problems
What Parents and Teachers can do

JUNE MARIE SCHASRE

Walker and Company • New York

First published in the United States of America in 1978 by the Walker Publishing Company, Inc.

Published simultaneously in Canada by Beaverbooks, Limited, Pickering, Ontario

ISBN: 0-8027-9052-6

Library of Congress Catalog Card Number: 77-26349

Printed in the United States of America

10 9 8 7 6 5 4 3 2 1

CONTENTS

FOREWORD

Perhaps you know a child who has been behaving oddly, and you wonder what could be the trouble. You want to help, but you feel uncertain about what to do. You may suspect that the child is trying to tell you something through his actions; yet you do not fully understand the meaning of his symptoms, and you find yourself reluctant to do anything that might make matters worse.

Countless teachers, parents, grandparents and guardians find themselves in situations such as this. All normal children behave oddly at times; just because a child does so occasionally need not be a cause for alarm. Nevertheless, some odd behavior can indicate the presence of emotional or physical disorders. The earlier the signs are recognized, and the sooner remedial action is taken, the better chance an affected child has of developing into a well-adjusted person.

As a teacher, I have encountered hundreds of young children over a period of years. Most of them have demonstrated their ability to adjust to childhood situations, indicating that they will in all probability grow up to become healthy, useful adults, able to cope with the problems of living, to hold down jobs, get along with others and function comfortably under reasonable pressures.

Occasionally, however, in my ordinary, everyday, average classroom, I have come into contact with children whose unusual behavior was clearly an appeal for help. With the assistance and advice of specialists such as child psychologists, psychiatrists, doctors, social workers, and remedial teachers, I have learned to recognize symptoms of a wide variety of disorders. By learning how to apply some basic principles of behavioral psychology, I have had a part in helping many of the troubled children in my classroom.

In working with problem children and discussing their distressing circumstances with their parents, it occurred to me that I might share some of their experiences with others who are responsible for the care and well being of children. In that respect, you may find this book a practical guide to helping a child.

You will learn how to alert yourself to a child's symptoms, and to understand what may be causing them. By understanding the dynamics of child growth and personality development, you can become better equipped to deal with such problems. Because pressures of one form or another are so widely responsible for many problems, I have included ways to relieve such pressures and to provide constructive outlets for a child's energies.

As you read about children and their various problems, you might be able to identify some aspect of their disturbances with a specific child's trouble. By seeing how symptoms were recognized and what specific measures were taken, you might glean some useful ideas and incorporate them into a child's actual situation. Your own common sense and experience, of course, will often be helpful. Nevertheless, when taking action to help a child, it can be reassuring to know how others, who have been faced with similar problems, have solved them successfully.

If a problem requires more than you feel able to handle, you can learn how and where to find professional assistance. In many cases, I have listed specific agencies for this purpose. If you wish to pursue a topic further, or from another viewpoint, I have included a list of recommended reading, consisting of books which are generally available at most public libraries or local bookstores.

Helping Children
with Problems

chapter 1

You and the Child

Tommy picked at his breakfast. His eyes looked feverish. He complained of a severe headache. In a short time he became too sick to go to school, so his mother tucked him into bed.

She went outside to wave the school bus past the house. When she returned, Tommy was out of bed, watching television in the living room with his younger brother. Both boys were eating doughnuts, and Tommy looked perfectly well.

Ordinarily, Tommy's mother would have been happy that he had recovered so quickly. However, Tommy had acted this way more and more in the last few months, and always on school days. His mother felt that he might be faking illness to avoid school.

On one earlier occasion, she had forced him onto the bus in spite of his complaints. Later that day, the school nurse telephoned to say that Tommy had a fever and virus. When his mother drove to the school to pick him up, the nurse's attitude showed what she thought of a mother who would send a sick child to school.

Tommy's mother did not want to repeat that mistake. Now, whenever he showed symptoms of sickness, she took no chances. It seemed safer to let him stay home.

She told herself that missing a few days of second grade would do him no harm. He was a bright boy, capable of catching up to the other children in his class. Nevertheless, she was puzzled and upset by his odd behavior.

The above incident is true. It concerned one of my pupils.

What does it mean when a child behaves oddly? If the behavior occurs only once or twice, the answer is, "Probably nothing." Children often see things differently from adults. Actions that seem reasonable to us may seem silly to a child; just as behavior that seems unreasonable to us may be completely sensible to a child.

However, if the behavior persists, as in Tommy's case, something may be wrong. The exaggerated reaction may be a distress signal. It is as though the child were saying, "Something is wrong. I can't help myself. Please help me!"

What can you do about it? The first thing is to become alert to the child's signals and to learn to distinguish them from normal conduct. This is easier than it might seem, if you keep in mind that children and adults alike tend to behave rationally most of the time. Hence, any repeated irrational action may be a distress signal.

Most signals hint at current problems, while some indicate future troubles. A child, for example, may throw a temper tantrum whenever he is not allowed to have his own way. As long as he is in the care of permissive persons, he may manage well enough—at least from his standpoint. However, he is headed for disaster when he grows older, for he will have to deal with people who are not impressed by his rages. For this reason, it is important to recognize any signs of unusual behavior as early as possible.

Once you have observed a distress signal, the next step is to interpret it. If you know why a child behaves as he does, it is usually possible to find a satisfactory remedy. Interpretation of distress signals is more difficult than simply recognizing them because it requires an understanding of child behavior. Essentially, that is what this book is about.

Distress signals take many forms and have numerous causes. Their diversity can cover a wide range. The task of making a diagnosis, therefore, may at first seem formidable. However, when you consider a great number of children with a wide variety of problems, patterns begin to emerge. You may then be able to see some of the ways children react to problems that they cannot solve for themselves.

This book contains the stories of 20 children and their problems. They have been chosen to present as wide a variety as possible. Let us look at Tommy's trouble more closely.

Tommy's illness was his distress signal. What was it about school that made him show symptoms of illness? As I was Tommy's teacher, his mother decided to see me in an effort to find a reason for his behavior.

When we discussed the situation, we both agreed that

2

Tommy was an intelligent boy whose work was generally satis-factory. I commented that his work was "almost perfect."

I then consulted Tommy's attendance record, which indi-cated that his absences followed a pattern. Because he became sick every other Thursday, and because spelling tests were given on Thursdays, I felt that his symptoms might be a way to avoid the tests.

"But he's good at spelling!" his mother insisted. "Everyone in our family always got *A* in spelling."

As tactfully as I could, I explained how a child could feel under pressure when he was forced to live up to family expec-tations. Although Tommy was good at spelling, he may have wanted to be perfect in order to gain his parents' approval.

As a result of his inability to accomplish this goal, he may have become apprehensive. His sickness would then have been a convenient way out of an unpleasant situation. Absence from school would have become a good excuse for not taking the test. In that way, he would not be letting anyone down.

Of course, Tommy would not think about it like that. On those test days, his head actually throbbed and the sick feelings were real. In other words, he was not lying. He did not say to himself, "Today is Thursday. There's a test in school which I'm afraid to take so I'll get sick and then I'll have to stay home. In that way, no one can criticize me." His body said all that for him; his sickness was his distress signal.

If that were the case, we had located the cause of his trouble. Tommy's problem could be solved by removing some of the pressure. I decided to let him take trial tests so that he would know exactly what to expect. I explained to him that tests are used to find out which words need further study. In that way, I hoped he would realize that I was trying to help him attain his goals.

His mother agreed to encourage him at home by giving him positive comments when he showed her a spelling paper. In-stead of saying, "Why did you have to get one word wrong?" she made remarks such as, "How nice that you got so many words right!"

Furthermore, we showed Tommy that neither of us was per-fect in spelling. For example, we occasionally made a point of looking up the spelling of a tricky word in a dictionary. When

Tommy saw that we, too, had trouble with some words, he began to accept his own shortcomings.

As with many solutions to problems, our approach was experimental. We were not specialists in child psychology; yet, we felt that some common sense might produce the desired results. After a reasonable interval, Tommy became less apprehensive about his spelling, but he continued to become sick on Thursdays.

I decided to examine his class record more closely. There were several instances when Tommy had been considered "uncooperative" during art lessons. The days when the art classes were scheduled coincided with Tommy's absences. Upon reflection, I recalled entering the art room and finding Tommy sitting in a corner reading a book. At that time, I had concluded that Tommy was not artistic and preferred reading to art.

However, I wished to check into any "coincidences" which could explain his behavior, so I brought the situation to the attention of the school psychologist. In checking with the art teacher, the psychologist discovered that Tommy was awkward with art materials, especially with scissors. Tommy had never completed an art project, nor was any of his work on display in the art room. This suggested that Tommy's absences could be related to his incompetence in art.

After fully examining the aspects of Tommy's problem, the psychologist agreed that the tensions surrounding spelling should be eased. He felt, however, that, as Tommy was present for some of the spelling tests, spelling was probably not the main reason for his trouble. The fact that he was sick almost every time the art class was scheduled promised to be more conclusive.

The psychologist suggested giving Tommy opportunities to experiment with numerous art materials so that he could experience some success in order to develop his confidence. Apparently, Tommy felt discouraged by his inability to use such materials, and rather than make something that would be rejected or ridiculed, he refused to try.

Tommy's mother obtained some materials, such as paint, paste and scissors. After she gave Tommy enough time to experiment with them on his own, she encouraged him to show his little brother how to use them. He felt superior to the younger child, and thus was not afraid to try out materials in front of him. If he made mistakes, his brother would not be aware of the fact.

During Tommy's free time in school, I made sure that he was directed toward the handwork center. Because he had previously avoided that part of the classroom, I worked directly with him to prevent him from wandering away. When he first began to manipulate scissors, his motions were awkward. I did not expect too much in the beginning. We just had fun together "making a mess" out of old magazines by cutting the pages into confetti. That gave him little trouble, for the shapes did not have to be perfect. The more Tommy cut, the more proficient he became.

No matter how much mess he made with the materials, I did not criticize him, but rather praised even his most rudimentary attempts. According to the psychologist, an important aspect of the treatment was sincerity.

At first sight, you may feel that praise for work that you consider inadequate can never be sincere. Fortunately, this is not necessarily true. If you watch for opportunities, you can almost always find *something* to praise. It does not matter that the thing you praise is unimportant compared with the faults. Because you are trying to build the child's confidence in himself, praise on any point will suffice. Even when the child is merely cutting up paper to make confetti scraps, you could say, for instance, "My, you got these pieces nice and small!"

"Better" is a useful word in such instances. When a child works at anything for more than a few minutes, he is almost bound to improve in some way. "You're doing better, you're getting the pieces smaller and your cuts are straighter," could be used in a similar situation.

Continuous praise such as this may occasionally cause a particular child to become boastful, overconfident or careless. Consequently, you may wish to avoid such a reaction by checking it with mild criticism. "Yes, you made the pieces small, but I'm sure you can make your cuts straighter if you really try."

When Tommy's mother and I worked with him, we occasionally made an intentional mistake, discarded the material,

5

and started over. By setting an example, we helped show him that self-expression does not have to be perfect.

During our campaign to help Tommy, he continued to be absent from art lessons. At home he spent much of his "sick" time working with paper, paste and scissors. The psychologist, meanwhile, visited the art room to observe the teacher's approach to teaching art. The teacher urged the students to "express themselves," in the assumption that they had the basic skills with which to proceed.

This was her first assignment at the primary grade level; her previous experience had been in a junior high school. She was grateful when the psychologist helped her to review some basic needs of young children. Once she understood that Tommy needed direct guidance and supervision in every step of an art assignment, she was eager to help him, when or if he returned to school for an art lesson.

At home, Tommy produced an attractive mosaic. The accomplishment excited him so much that he took the design along when he visited the psychologist for a follow-up interview. The psychologist asked if he might borrow it to hang in his office for everyone to admire. Of course Tommy was proud to let his work go on display.

Unknown to Tommy, the art teacher was invited to the psychologist's office during one of Tommy's visits. When Tommy saw her, he seemed apprehensive, obviously associating her with failure and disappointment. When she looked at the design and asked who made it, though, her tone of approval led Tommy to boast, "I did!"

She complimented him and suggested making some mosaics during the next art period.

"They might to too difficult for the other kids," she told Tommy. "Would you please help me show the kids how to make them?"

Needless to say, Tommy was eager to attend the next art class. He could now look forward to it with pleasure instead of pain, for he was sure of succeeding and thus not afraid to try. Furthermore, he was confident that he would not be criticized by the other children.

Tommy's status was established among his classmates by the fact that he was able to help them with a worthwhile project.

He began to feel important in his social group. His feelings of uselessness gradually disappeared, and by the end of the year, his attendance at school was satisfactory.

COMMENTS

I have used Tommy's story to show you how a problem can cause a child to send out a distress signal. You have seen how common sense can help you recognize the signal. Knowledge of child behavior can help you investigate, and thereby understand, some of the reasons for such signals.

Further, I have attempted to point out methods of remedy. Thus by reading Tommy's story, you can learn how problems may be solved. In Tommy's case, prompt recognition and careful guidance helped him overcome his problem.

We saw that Tommy's problem was caused by *pressure* that he was not mature enough to handle by himself. Pressures of one sort or another can cause a variety of symptoms from stammering to nose bleeds. As you read through this book, you will see many cases in which pressure was the cause, or at least a contributing cause, of the child's distress.

In order to relieve pressure, you must first find its cause. In Tommy's case, spelling was an obvious source of pressure. However, we had to do a little detective work to learn that his failure to cope with art materials was the real root of the matter.

Once we learned that Tommy had a "pressure" problem and determined what caused it, we were able to apply several remedies. These were fairly simple. One or more of them can be helpful in almost every "pressure" case.

We avoided criticism. Tommy's standard of success was reduced from an unattainable "perfection" to a level that he was well able to reach. We demonstrated *by example* that failure to reach perfection was less serious than he had believed.

We provided tasks that he could accomplish with credit. His successes were praised. Furthermore, Tommy was given opportunities to acquire status among his peers by helping them with tasks where he was superior.

Tommy's case may have nothing to do with what is troubling a child with whom you are concerned. However, you will be wise to acquaint yourself with a great variety of problems and possible solutions. In doing so, you make yourself ready for any situation that you may have to deal with in the future.

Then, when a child acts oddly, you can call upon your reserves of knowledge to help you understand the situation. Children have a way of doing the unexpected. When some action catches you off guard, you may respond emotionally. You may be angry, impatient or disappointed. That is natural, but by following your own instincts at such a time, you may do harm rather than good.

Most children's problems are fairly simple. Unfortunately, some are more complicated and require professional help. The examples in my stories will show ways to get such help.

In some instances, you may find that a child's problem seems to fit one of the stories exactly. If this is the case, keep in mind that, in fact, there may be important differences. No two children are exactly alike. For this reason, you will be wise to acquaint yourself with the wide range covered by all the stories. By doing this, you will understand how problems in general are handled, and thus help prepare for any problems that may occur in the future.

For example, a particular child may be overactive. You could be tempted to read only the story about hyperkinetic children. Of course you might learn much by doing this. Nevertheless, by overlooking the other stories, you might miss an important clue to that child's total behavior, present and future.

Let's say the child does not stutter; thus you skip the story about a stammering child. However, the underlying condition causing the signal could be similar to a problem confronting the child with whom you are concerned. That child could have the same basic problem as the stutterer but express his signal in a different form: Instead of stuttering, he might wet the bed or bite his fingernails.

By learning as much as you can about the greatest variety of signals given by many children, you will better equip yourself to deal with any child's problems when they occur.

You may actually recognize yourself as a child in some of the stories. In that sense, reading through the book could be a form of therapy in helping you to understand yourself.

Tommy's story is true. However, those that follow are composite. Although the incidents really happened, I have combined the cases of children with similar problems, and I have omitted facts that concerned only one child. This has let me make the stories simpler, easier to understand and more general. It has also enabled me to conceal the identies of the children who were actually involved. The names I have given them are fictitious.

—————— RECOMMENDED READING

Doll, Ronald C. *Children Under Pressure*. Columbus, Ohio: C.E. Merrill Books, 1966

Gaudry, Eric and Charles D. Spielberger. *Anxiety and Educational Achievement*. New York: Wiley, 1971

Gray, Jeffrey Alan. *The Psychology of Fear and Stress*. New York: McGraw-Hill, 1971.

Hill, Kennedy T. *Test Anxiety*. Chicago: University of Chicago Press, 1966

Phillips, Beeman N. *Anxiety and School-Related Interventions*. Albany: University of the State of New York, Division of Research, 1971.

Varma, Ved P. *Stresses in Children*. New York: Crane Russak, 1973.

chapter 2

Sarah

(A PROBLEM OF STRESS)

Sarah stuttered whenever she became excited. She was such a nervous child that she stammered most of the time.

Before she began school, her problem did not affect her too deeply. Even in kindergarten, she was able to get along with other children because the activities there could be carried on without much talk.

When she reached first grade, and tried to read aloud, her stuttering caused the other children to giggle or snicker. Their reaction led Sarah to withdraw into herself and talk only when it was absolutely necessary. Sometimes she refused to talk at all.

Consequently, most people considered her stubborn. When her classmates were reading, Sarah retreated behind a bookcase where it appeared that she was sulking. She refused to participate in the usual classroom activities, such as Show and Tell, word games or singing. When asked to give an answer to a question, she generally shrugged her shoulders or ignored the request entirely.

Eventually, Sarah became a real problem in the classroom. One day, I noticed her sitting by herself at a table, counting beads. A little girl named Debbie, who was a slow learner, sat down alongside her and began working with the beads. Suddenly Sarah grabbed Debbie's hands and shoved them aside in a rude fashion. When Debbie pushed back, it became a fight.

After putting a stop to it, I asked the girls what had happened. Debbie accused Sarah of "picking on her." Sarah turned a sullen face away from me, and clenched her fists as if she wanted to hit Debbie. There was an expression on her face that suggested more than anger. At that moment it became apparent that Sarah was an unhappy child and that her stuttering was obviously a distress signal.

Did she stutter because she was upset, or did she get upset over her stuttering? Was there some physical reason for her stammering, or did she have an emotional problem? I decided to check out the physical aspect first by consulting the school's speech therapist.

He tested her and found that she was able to talk without stuttering, provided that she was alone with him and he gave her sufficient time to speak. If other children were present, she either stuttered or refused to say anything.

As it was obvious that her problem was not physical, I asked the school psychologist to interview her. The psychologist's schedule was busy; Sarah's problem was less serious than some of the others; so her name was placed on a waiting list. Meanwhile, the psychologist suggested avoiding situations that would upset her.

It was difficult to determine what upset Sarah because she lived in a high-pitched key. For example, when I read a story to the children, Sarah overreacted. If the story was amusing, she laughed uproariously, long after the other children had stopped; if it was sad, she sobbed loudly.

At last her parents met with the psychologist. Sarah's mother and father were talkative, impatient people who, during the entire interview, looked at their wristwatches frequently. When the psychologist directed a question at Sarah, one of her parents answered it for her. It became obvious that Sarah rarely had an opportunity to speak at home.

The psychologist discussed this with Sarah's parents, explaining how important it is for a child to have an adult's complete attention occasionally. Evidently, Sarah's opportunity for doing this was rare. When she did have a chance to talk, she tried to say too much. Consequently she talked too fast, her words became jumbled, and she worried about running out of time. This made her so nervous that the stuttering pattern developed and ultimately grew worse.

Her parents had not realized what was happening. They were accustomed to her stuttering. Because they were impatient, and saved time for her by finishing words she tried to say, she rarely had a chance to speak for herself without being interrupted. Over a period of time, the stuttering became a habit and, as with most habits, it was easier to acquire than to eliminate.

This information enabled us to work out a program designed to help Sarah. It started at home with her parents. The first step was to enlighten them tactfully. When they realized that Sarah's stuttering was a distress signal, they were eager to cooperate. They were given some suggestions that I consider worthy of being repeated here. Teachers, confronted by a similar problem, may wish to offer such ideas to concerned parents.

1. Spend some time alone each day with the child. Be sure it is every day, rather than a saved-up interval such as a weekend or brief, concentrated vacation. A child lives in the present. His current needs must be met on that basis.

2. Give the child your full attention. For example, do not wash the dishes, sew, fill your pipe, pet the dog or engage in a simultaneous activity while dealing with the child. Meet the child face to face. When a child wants to give you his attention, he usually looks directly into your face. Give him the same courtesy.

3. Let the child do most of the talking. Many children do not have sufficient opportunity to really talk to adults. Get the conversation going with a question or two, but avoid "quizzing" the child.

4. Be a good listener. What a child says may bore you, especially if it is a detailed description of a television show or something of that nature. However, if you care about the child and his emotional and intellectual progress, he does not bore you. On the contrary, a study of the child's mind can be fascinating. What did he notice? What did he overlook? What made him laugh? What annoyed him? When you listen in this way, a whole new world may open up for you. You may not become an expert in child psychology, but you will become knowledgeable in the psychological development of the child.

5. Never use this time for correction, discipline or criticism. Let it be a time for accepting the child for what

12

he is. If the child regards your time together as p
ment, he will come to hate it. However, if he is
pletely accepted as an interesting individual, he
look forward to it eagerly.

6. In addition to your private time with the child, try to include him in as many ordinary activities as possible. For example, ask his opinion during a dinner table conversation. Encourage a comment during a television show, a shopping trip or a drive in the car.

7. If you feel that you have no time, find it. This can be done by closely examining your daily activities. Surely there are five or 10 minutes in each 24-hour interval that you can set aside for a child who is important to you.

8. This is mentioned last, but may be the most important of all. Do not fall into the trap of telling yourself that your child is different and does not need such attention. No matter how happy and busy the child may seem to be, he needs individual attention from an adult every day. Some children need less than others, but all children need it and thrive on it.

Be careful not to overdo it by giving the child too much attention. That could create a self-centered personality. There seems to be little danger of this, since today's children need much attention. If we give it to them in constructive ways, perhaps they will not need to send out their distress signals.

The above list of suggestions has been copied by many teachers whom I know, and given to parents as a reference and reminder. Most interested parents will readily accept concrete suggestions of this nature.

After discussing the situation with Sarah's parents, the next step was to work with her in the classroom. I tried to let Sarah experience success in talking in front of the other children. It was done indirectly, by involving her in theatrical play in the hope that she would escape from herself momentarily by becoming someone else.

We set up a small stage with a curtain to hide behind. Four or five children could kneel behind it and operate hand puppets, all the while making up stories to be acted out. The characters "talked" through the children's voices.

At first Sarah merely watched the shows. One day I took her aside and asked her if she would like to be the queen puppet. I reminded her that queens were important people, and that everyone had to listen to a queen and obey her commands.

Assured that the queen would get the full attention of the other puppets, as well as of the audience, Sarah accepted the part. Once behind the curtain, she lost her own identity, became the queen and did not stutter. The children listened and applauded as the queen puppet bowed. After the performance, a happy Sarah emerged from behind the curtain.

During the weeks that followed, Sarah still did not join in the reading groups, but continued to retreat to her favorite spot behind the bookcase. However, I noticed that she now took a puppet with her and invented new plots for future shows. She was no longer restless and disruptive while the other children were reading, for she had something interesting to do with her time.

She began telling me her stories, and I started writing down her words. Eventually, she was encouraged to read some of her stories aloud, which she was able to do without stuttering. It was obvious that she was a good reader, and the children asked for her help with words.

As a means to interest Sarah in joining a reading group, I appointed her a helper. Even though she still stuttered, the children began to overlook it. They seemed to sense that she had something worthwhile to say, and they were willing to give her their attention.

Her duties as a helper eventually took her to the math table. I discovered that she had not "picked on" Debbie, but had wanted to help her solve a problem. Debbie was a slow learner, while Sarah was fast to grasp numerical concepts. Sarah's parents had set the example which she followed—she interrupted someone to help him. Thus, she had reached over to remove the beads from a classmate's hands in order to use them to show Debbie the right answer to a math problem. Because Sarah had not said anything as she did so, both Debbie and I had misunderstood her gesture.

Two years have passed since Sarah was in my classroom.

14

She is a different child now, with few emotional outbursts. When she became able to speak without stuttering, she no longer needed her old way of communicating. Her uncontrolled laughing or crying had been a convenient way to express herself.

Sarah became able to communicate as she gained self-confidence. Her parents found time to give her the attention she needed. Sarah knew that they would listen to her.

Sarah's positive school experiences also helped her have more self-confidence. Because she felt needed and accepted by the other children, she began to consider herself a worthwhile individual.

All of these reactions worked together to stop her stuttering. The distress signal was seen, its cause was discovered and positive steps were taken to solve Sarah's problem. With teachers and parents working together, Sarah has become a happy child.

COMMENTS

Children stutter for a variety of reasons. In some cases, the cause is physical; in others, it is emotional. When physical factors have been ruled out, emotional factors should be sought.

The underlying cause may be stress or strain. Sometimes simple shyness causes children to stutter. Fear of failure or lack of confidence may also be contributing causes. Some children overstrive and, as a result of the tensions which accompany this, they often blurt out their words in a stammering way.

In my experience, one of the most common causes of stuttering may well be the unwillingness of adults to permit children to speak freely. Many children are told to "be quiet" or "shut up" while adults are conversing. Thus, when they finally have a chance to say anything, they try to get as much out as possible in the time allowed. This may be one cause of stammering, especially in sensitive children.

You may be interested in trying a simple diagnostic test to seek a possible cause of stuttering. It was suggested to me by a person whose opinions I respect and who has had experience with amateur actors. At least some actors, and even professional singers, sometimes stutter when they try to talk. Because they can *perform* without stuttering, it means that the problem cannot be in either the speech control area of the brain or in the vocal mechanism.

Correction of the problem may be difficult, but a diagnostic test is easy. Have the child memorize a brief poem, and ask him to recite it when you are alone with him and when he is under no pressure. If his stutter disappears or is greatly improved, you have eliminated at least one possible source of the trouble.

The important thing to realize is that stammering, or any other distress signal the child shows, is brought about by a situation that the child cannot tolerate or handle. When the situation is changed, the distress signal often ceases.

Many "tension" situations may lead to disturbance-based habits such as stuttering, nail biting or thumb-sucking. One example of a tension situation is a naturally left-handed person being forced to use his right hand. This sometimes creates emotional tension which may lead to various disturbances, that, in turn, produce habits such as mentioned above.

A child is actually relieving the tension by engaging in the habit. We can help the child overcome the habit by finding other ways to relieve his tensions. Simply letting the child talk, and giving him enough time to be heard, as in Sarah's case, often proves helpful.

Stuttering and such habits are regarded as manifestations of the child's total personality rather than an isolated disturbance. Whenever possible, therefore, think in terms of the total child. Give him opportunities to express himself freely, take time to listen, and let him feel that he is an important individual. Give him as much encouragement as you can, for a discouraged child is a child with a problem.

Let him escape from himself now and then. Children love to pretend. Give the child a chance to become someone else, the way Sarah became the queen puppet. Finger puppets, costumes, wigs or a simple paper hat often help change the identity of a child momentarily, long enough to help him overcome his problem for a brief interval.

When allowing children to trade roles with each other, try to avoid selecting partners who have undersirable habits. In Sarah's case, for example, Debbie might have traded places with Sarah. She might have worn Sarah's sweater and begun stuttering. This would be undesirable for two reasons: It would point up Sarah's inadequacies and hurt her feelings, and it would encourage Debbie to develop an unwanted habit. To be sure Sarah was included in such games, I tried to encourage her partner to imitate her pleasing, positive traits, such as the graceful way she moved when she danced.

It is most important to refrain from interrupting a stuttering child. This calls attention to his condition and tends to make it worse by overemphasizing it. Instead, try to give realistic, constructive suggestions to the child. If you let the child know that you are genuinely interested in him as an individual, he will become more receptive to your help.

——— RECOMMENDED READING

Burger, Isabel B. *Creative Play Acting*. New York: Ronald Press, 1966.

Emerick, Lon L. *An Analysis of Stuttering*. Danville, Ill.: Interstate Printers & Publishers, 1972.

———. *Therapy for Young Stutterers*. Danville, Ill.: Interstate Printers & Publishers, 1970.

Moses, Gerald R. *Readings in Speech Disfluency*. New York: MSS Information Corp., 1972.

Moustakes, Clark E. *Children in Play Therapy*. New York: J. Aronson, 1973.

Sheehan, Joseph Green. *Stuttering, Research and Therapy*. New York: Harper & Row, 1970.

Van Riper, Charles Gage. *The Nature of Stuttering*. Englewood Cliffs, N.J.: Prentice-Hall, 1971.

chapter 3

Andy
(A PROBLEM OF PHYSICAL AND PSYCHOLOGICAL HANDICAP)

Andy appeared to be a typical "daydreamer." His attention wandered during lessons. He had a faraway expression in his eyes that suggested secret thoughts. When called upon to answer questions, he seldom responded.

He was a tall boy for a 10-year-old; consequently, he was assigned a desk in the rear of the classroom. He took advantage of being out of my immediate vicinity by disturbing the children who sat near him. While they wrote their assignments, Andy nudged them or tossed bits of eraser at them.

When I gave directions, he wandered over to the pencil sharpener, or looked out the window. He rarely understood what to do. Whenever I asked him why he had not finished an assignment, he shrugged his shoulders and grinned sheepishly. I became annoyed at his habit of answering, "Huh?" to everything I asked him.

His school records indicated that his intelligence was about "normal." As ours was a heterogeneous group, that put him near the upper middle of the others; yet he did not seem to learn very much.

The fact that he failed most of his tests worried his parents, for their other children were bright and ambitious. During an interview with Andy's father, I learned that Andy rarely listened at home.

"All he does is watch TV with the volume turned up," he said. "We have to yell at him to turn it down."

His remark made me wonder if Andy could be hard of hearing. Upon reflection, I recalled several instances when I was

18

positive he did not hear me. When I asked his father about it, he replied, "He can hear all right. He just doesn't listen."

Andy's father went on to explain that the boy was capable of eavesdropping. "If he can hear us whispering about his birthday present, he isn't deaf!" he commented.

Nevertheless, I obtained his father's permission to have Andy tested by the school's audio-technician. The tests showed that Andy had a slight hearing impairment in his right ear. A physical examination was then scheduled to ascertain the cause of the trouble.

Meanwhile, we moved Andy's desk close to the front of the room where he was positioned with his good ear close to the place where I customarily stood while giving verbal directions.

The audio-technician suggested that I call Andy's name before saying anything to him to get his attention. Once I had his attention, I hoped he would be inclined to listen more carefully. This proved difficult because I have a soft voice. To avoid straining my voice by shouting his name, I devised a system to capture his attention without speaking.

Because he watched television so frequently, he was visually oriented. Therefore, something that he could see would be likely to attract his attention. I made a set of identity cards, consisting of 4″ × 4″ cards on which I printed each child's initials. I held up the cards while lessons were in progress. The children found them a fair way of choosing who would answer questions, who would have first turn in line, who would choose partners and so on.

By shuffling the cards, I could place the responsibility of choice upon Fate rather than my own personal preferences. Thus there were no favorites, and all of the children became more attentive as they watched the cards. Because the entire class was involved, Andy did not feel handicapped. The visual challenge of looking for his card encouraged him to be more attentive. In addition to helping Andy, I was able to reach some of the shy children who had been nondescript faces in the classroom.

Although Andy seemed to hear farily well on some days, most of the time he showed signs of deep concentration, suggesting that he was straining to hear what I was saying. He obviously needed help with his work, even though he was beginning to pay attention to the activities in the classroom.

As a means of giving Andy assistance, I asked the children to select "study buddies." During their work time, two children sat together. When one child did not understand (or hear) the directions, his partner could explain and assist. The brighter, faster learners had an opportunity to help the slower learners. This enhanced the feeling of Andy's being no different from the others, as well as proving helpful to the total learning situation.

Because Andy had several good days when his hearing was satisfactory, I asked the audio-technician to retest him. The second test turned out completely normal in both ears. By that time, Andy had seen a physician, who found Andy's tonsils enlarged and infected. His frequent sore throats, sinus "colds" and swollen glands seemed to be responsible for intermittent bouts of impaired hearing.

The school nurse mentioned that this is fairly common in children, as well as adults. During or after a cold or sinus infection, a person often has "ringing" in the ears from changes in pressure. The fact that Andy had infected tonsils possibly could explain his temporary inability to hear well.

We made plans to have Andy tested at regular intervals. Once or twice during the tests he had trouble hearing, even though he did not have a sign of a cold or swollen glands. The school psychologist suggested that it may have been caused by nervousness or excitement.

Any number of emotions, he explained, may cause a person to experience impaired hearing, sight or any other sense. For example, we are familiar with the terms "blind rage" or "seeing red" when a person becomes so furious that he is unable to see the world as it actually is. This can happen to one's hearing capacity as well. We become frightened and our hearts pound in our ears, shutting out all other sounds for a moment. In this sense, Andy's problem was psychological as well as physical.

During spring recess, Andy had his tonsils removed. His bouts of swollen glands subsided. He no longer had a ringing in his ears, yet he still had trouble hearing. I recalled his father's words: "He can hear, but he doesn't *listen!*"

Because listening is a difficult skill to acquire, requiring training and experience, we began a program to induce good listening habits. During an interval each day, we moved visual objects from the classroom. A simultaneous program was begun at Andy's home with full cooperation of his parents.

Definite times were set aside for looking and other times were reserved for listening. Instead of looking at books or watching television, Andy was encouraged to listen to a tape recorder. We decided that this would be more interesting and challenging than a record player because it involved his own voice. He sang or talked into the microphone and then listened to the playback.

Other children participated by creating a sound effects game. They taped various sounds, such as a bike horn, whistle, doorbell, clock ticking, dog barking and many more. Then they asked other children to listen to the sounds and guess what they were. Because some of the sounds were faint, it was a good way to monitor Andy's ability to hear low intensity sounds.

Andy's father carried the process a fascinating step further. He bought a citizens' band radio and began sending and receiving messages. As a reward for good school work, Andy was allowed to participate in the C.B. program, in which his code name became "Handy Andy." His overpowering interest in television waned. He began talking more and listening more. By the end of the school year, he had no hearing problem.

--------------------------------- COMMENTS

All cases of impaired hearing or sight are not as simple as Andy's. However, the basic elements of his problem exist in many cases.

Andy's inattention, for example, was one clue to his problem. Many children are inattentive because they simply do not hear or see too well. Thus, it is wise to have a child tested as early as possible for such impairment.

Until an expert can test a child's hearing, there are some

ways of monitoring the child's ability. Here, for example, are some things to watch for when you suspect a child may be hard of hearing:

1. Does he fail to respond when you call his name, especially if his back is toward you?
2. Does he give the impression of daydreaming?
3. Does he cock his head to one side while listening?
4. Does he talk in unusually loud tones? This is not to be confused with the normal shouting of active children at play.
5. Does he speak with a sing-song quality?
6. Does he talk in a monotone?
7. Is he unable to carry a tune or tell which sound is higher or lower than another?
8. Does he consistently ask you to repeat directions, or fail to carry out instructions?

While any or all of these may be indications of other problems, nevertheless, it is advisable to suspect a hearing problem before looking further.

Once the child's hearing is found to be impaired, there are many ways to handle the situation. A child with such a handicap, at least in milder forms, will certainly profit from a relationship with normal children as long as he is not made to feel conspicuous. By including others in activities designed to help the child, you can create an atmosphere in which he will be able to free himself of tensions and frustrations that may otherwise deter him.

The visual cue cards, for example, included all of the children in the classroom. This enabled Andy to cope with his problem without feeling that he was different.

Of course, any child with a severe disability will do best in a situation where he will receive specialized attention and training. Borderline cases such as Andy's, though, seem to profit most by "being with the gang."

It is most important for teachers to remember to make a note of the problem on the child's record. Busy teachers, especially those in upper grade levels with several classes and hundreds of students each day, often do not have the time to give record cards ample scrutiny.

Therefore, a teacher will be helpful if the entry on the child's record card is made as boldly as possible. If it can be noted at a glance, a future teacher, busy as can be, will surely see it and be alerted to the problem. It could well prevent a child from being mistaken for a daydreamer or a behavior problem.

Parents should be encouraged to notify the teacher about their child's limitations. They may send a note or make an early appointment to discuss the problem with the teacher, especially if the child transfers to a new school. Records generally follow the child, often in a roundabout and slothful way, and tend to appear too late to help in diagnosing the child.

If the exact nature of the problem is not known, such a parent-teacher conference at least can bring to light the existence of a problem. Consequently, a specialist, such as an audio-technician or school nurse, can be consulted as soon as possible.

Andy's father was partially correct in assuming that Andy did not listen. Andy had gradually developed a habit of tuning out various sounds. This was in part a result of his actual inability to hear when his glands were swollen, and further magnified by the fact that his parents yelled at him instead of trying to find other ways to capture his attention.

When his problem was identified, corrective measures were taken. In summary, here are some positive ways in which you may help a child in a similar situation:

1. Decide what the child is interested in. Use this to capture his attention. Andy liked watching television; watching the identity cards became a substitute activity and enabled him to carry over a habit he enjoyed into a new situation.
2. When you have the child's attention, keep it by adding interest and variety. In Andy's case, we prevented his interest in the tape recorder from diminishing by augmenting it with the C.B. radio experience. The fact that the latter was given as a reward acted as a motivating factor.

3. Try to include other children in the experience. Friends, classmates, brothers and sisters will enjoy sharing the fun. This will help prevent the impaired child from feeling isolated or different.

As I mentioned before, any of the senses can be faulty. Impaired vision is even more common than loss of hearing. Children who are poor readers or writers may be unable to see clearly. An eye examination and prescription lenses often work wonders in such cases. But before going to the expense of consulting an eye doctor, you may look for some signs of possible vision troubles. These are:

1. Squinting.
2. Headaches.
3. Watering eyes.
4. Frequent rubbing of the eyes.
5. Holding books in unusual positions.
6. Turning the head sideways while looking at objects or while reading.
7. Sensitivity to bright light.
8. Staring into space or having a "blank" expression.
9. Poor hand-to-eye coordination.
10. Inability to read or write despite efforts to teach the child.

Upon occasion we may fear that a child has a severe learning disability, when in reality the problem may be of a simple, physical nature. Thus, it is to a child's advantage to have him examined before attempting to make a judgment about his behavior.

———— RECOMMENDED READING

Duker, Samuel. *Teaching Listening in the Elementary School*. Metuchen, N.J.: Scarecrow Press, 1971.
Edgington, Dorothy. *The Physically Handicapped Child in Your Classroom*. (A Handbook for Teachers). Springfield, Ill.: C.C. Thomas, 1976.

Miller, Alfred L. *A Practical Guide on Hearing Impaired Children*. Springfield, Ill.: C.C. Thomas, 1970.

Moffat, Samuel. *Helping the Child Who Cannot Hear*. New York: Public Affairs Committee, 1972.

Wepman, Joseph M. *Auditory Discrimination Test*. Chicago: Language Research Associates, Inc., 1973.

Zigmond, Naomi K. *Auditory Learning*. San Raphael, Cal.: Dimensions, 1968.

chapter 4

Gary
(A PROBLEM OF TEMPORARY ABNORMALITY)

On registration day, a woman appeared at my second grade classroom door holding her son's hand. He was an oversized seven-year-old, weighing over 100 pounds, and more than a head taller than any of the other children in the class.

"Here's Gary," she announced, pushing him toward me and adding, "It will be a miracle if you can do anything with him!"

The boy looked ready to cry. Despite his near-adult size, he had a cherubic face and a young child's expression. He was a *big* little kid, a physical abnormality which, from the way his mother acted, had evidently caused some problems.

Testing in the previous grade had shown him to be a normally intelligent child. However, the tests had been done on a verbal level because he was unable to read the questions. For some reason he had been unable to learn to read. In such a case, a child is usually retained in first grade to give him more time to become ready for the reading experience. However, after much consideration, my school's administrative staff decided to promote Gary "on condition."

The promotion was obviously made in the boy's best interest, for his size seemed to create a bigger problem than his inability to read. A smaller child would have been given the advantage of another year of reading readiness, but it was thought that retention in first grade would upset Gary because he would feel out of place with the smaller children. The attitude of the children toward him, in turn, might prevent him from learning anything.

Gary giggled in a self-concious manner when a large, fifth-

26

grade desk was moved into the room to accommodate him. He sat down at the desk and began to scribble with crayons, all the while glancing at me out of the corner of his eye. I had the distinct feeling that he was waiting for something to happen.

Gary did not recognize his name when I printed it on the chalkboard, nor could he print it when I gave him paper and pencil. In fact, he could not hold the pencil in a position for printing, but rather gripped it and broke the point. Then he headed for the pencil sharpener and commenced to grind up the pencil.

During the week that followed, I noticed that Gary was not accepted by the other children. During their games, they excluded him, possibly because he was unintentionally rough. He seemed resigned to sit on the sidelines, scribbling with crayons or else operating the pencil sharpener.

Gary needed some kind of goal toward which to aim. As he liked to sharpen pencils and was good at using the pencil sharpener, I gave him a job. He became our pencil helper, and found satisfaction in doing something which the other children found difficult. His large hands were far more capable than theirs in handling the sharpener, and the children readily took their pencils to him when necessary.

There is a limit, however, to the number of pencils to be sharpened during the course of a day. Gary needed more activities to occupy his time, activities which must have meaning for him if they were to be useful to his development.

When I made an inventory of Gary's awareness of sound-to-symbol relationships, I discovered that he had difficulty in associating letters with the sounds they represented. Since that association is the basic skill needed in learning to read, I felt that he must be taught it in some way.

His job as pencil helper provided a good opportunity to try something new. I obtained pencils for everyone in the classroom. On the end of each child's pencil, I printed the first letter of that child's name. Gary, of course, knew his classmates by name. If he could learn to associate the form of a letter with the beginning sound of a name, he would be approaching a level of reading readiness.

The children were arranged in groups of six. I made sure that no group contained two children with the same beginning letter in his name. Then I put each group's pencils into separate cans and numbered the cans to correspond to the groups.

All Gary had to do was look at a can, note its number, and approach the corresponding group. When he called a child's name, that child would take his own pencil from Gary. I did not instruct Gary to distribute the pencils. This allowed him to "save face" because at that point he did not know whose pencils he was handling. Neither did I demand that he notice the letter on the pencil which he handed any child, for I hoped this would be a case of independent discovery.

My hopes were realized. Soon, for example, Gary began to choose David's pencil because it had a *D* on it. He had observed David selecting that particular pencil and eventually associated David with that letter.

When the pencils had been sharpened down to a small size, I took advantage of that fact in order to make a change in the procedure. I obtained new pencils and printed each child's entire first name on the end. Of course, I was fairly certain that Gary would look at only the first letter of each name, but at the same time, I hoped that he would unconsciously notice the whole word pattern and soon associate it with the child.

I allowed a sufficient interval for Gary to experience success and to feel confidence. Then I rearranged the children's seats into groups in which more than one child had the same first initial. Now Danny, as well as David, belonged to the same group. I rearranged the pencils in the cans to correspond to the new groupings, and asked Gary to distribute the pencils.

There were some mix-ups at first, but not for long. Gary soon learned to distinguish whole words and to differentiate between words with similar elements.

The phonetic elements in many of the names were similar to some words in the reading books, such as *car* and *Carl, Fred* and *red,* and so on. By seeing these elements in various ways, Gary began to recognize simple words.

I did not expect Gary to discover this similarity all by himself. Once it was demonstrated to him a few times, however, he seemed eager to go on with other sounds and symbols. Eventually, he began to read phrases and sentences. By the end of the school year, he had completed his first reader. That

was far below second grade level, but it was a great acc(
plishment for an individual who had been considered "untea(
able."

What is more, it was accomplished without direct reference
to Gary's difference in size or ability. The other children went
to him for help with their pencils; they, in turn, helped him to
read. His study partner took delight in going over words and
phrases with Gary.

When evaluating individual progress, the class often discussed "growing rates," which became one of Gary's favorite
subjects. In private, I explained to him that he was growing
more rapidly in body than the other children, but that they
would catch up to him some day, just as he was catching up to
their reading levels. This provided him with the encouragement
he needed, and he had enough confidence, and had developed
sufficient basic skills, to continue learning in his subsequent
situations.

—————————————— COMMENTS

Gary's problem was one of *temporary abnormality*. A child's
physcial appearance is a most important aspect of his total be-
havorial system. Any overly large child is at an immediate disadvantage because he appears older than others his age, and
people generally expect more of him. A seven-year-old who
looks 12 is not expected, for example, to cry, wet his pants or
play games enjoyed by much younger children.

A teacher or parent can help such a temporarily abnormal
child by encouraging him to perform tasks impossible for
smaller children. Some jobs a big child might perform with satisfaction are moving large objects about a room, raising and
lowering windows, writing near the top of the chalkboard, putting objects on high shelves, reaching items from top shelves in
classroom or market, using tools that require larger hands and
greater muscular power and so on.

Care should be taken, of course, to avoid having the child
feel that you are taking advantage of him because of his size.
If he dislikes a task, for instance, he should not be forced to do

it just because he is physically capable of performing it. This may lead to hostility toward other children who are not asked to do the task because they are smaller and, to him, of a more desirable size.

Assignments can be an unobtrusive way to produce the overture to learning just about anything. The method can be used in school or at home and in any subject. If a child needs help in math, he can be asked to carry enough chairs for the members of his reading group. He counts the children and the chairs, and begins to understand a one-to-one relationship in counting numbers. Likewise, further problems can be worked out by having him note how many more chairs are needed to accommodate a particular number of children. By actually seeing the children who have no chairs, he gets a concrete, useful picture in his mind. This is preferable to giving him an abstract number, which at this point in his development may be meaningless to him.

If a parent should ask a teacher how this can be carried out at home, the teacher might suggest having the child arrange chairs around a dinner table, counting the guests. Many tasks are attractive to a child because the activities are considered "grown-up."

It is important to refrain from taking the child for granted and using him as a "servant." After all, he is still a child and needs childish activities, such as active play and romping. Nevertheless, he needs to learn, and a good way to start is to give him meaningful tasks which he can accomplish with satisfaction. After each task is completed, a word of praise works wonders to help build the child's self-image and sense of worth.

Too much praise, on the other hand, can be harmful. The child might get the idea that he is superior to other children. At such times, you might offer a reminder that he is catching up to others in certain ways just as they are catching up to him in some ways.

Always begin with a simple project that you feel sure will give the child some success and let that success grow by assigning more complex tasks. Gary's sense of defeat was acute because he had rarely been successful at anything. Further, his mother felt that he was "unteachable." In a sense, he reflected her attitude. You, yourself, then, must have confidence in the child before he can acquire any of his own.

I do not hesitate to ask other children to help. Children are almost always willing to help one another when they know they will be rewarded. The reward need not be material, but may take the form of a compliment, or an extra privilege.

In Gary's case, I did not want the other children to feel inferior to *him*, either. I always made it clear that each individual grows, physically and mentally, at different rates, and in a matter of time, all will become adults. They understood this, and the relevancy of the situation made Gary's problem easier to handle.

Because Gary's problem was temporary, it was essential to help him believe that his condition would ultimately change. The fact that Gary was learning to read each day helped him to wait out his time, for he felt some immediate success in at least one area of his life. Waiting is a difficult occupation for a child, to whom a week, or even a few days, often seems forever. Long range plans, therefore, tend to frustrate most children. Whenever possible, then, try to have the child engage in an activity that he realizes is helping him in the present.

If you can, minimize the differences between children whenever possible. In Gary's case, his parents were advised to look for similarities. One of Gary's friends was interested in walkie-talkie radios. When Gary became interested in that manner of communicating, he began to spend time with his friend, despite the fact that the other boy was unusually small. Both boys seemed to sense the fact that the activity in which they were interested could be carried on by a person of any size; thus their size was of no significance in their relationship.

As some children are overweight, rather than oversized, their increased poundage can be controlled by diet. Overeating is generally the basic cause of overweight. With today's emphasis on "junk foods" or TV snacks, many children eat too much.

Overweight at any age can be a potential health hazard. In a child, it can lead to psychological problems as well. No child wants to be called "Fatty" by classmates and friends. I have found that girls are usually more self-conscious about their

31

weight and can thus be induced to accept a restricted diet more readily than boys.

Before attempting to suggest that a child go on a diet, it is wise to recommend that the child be examined by a physician to determine the cause of his overweight. Overeating may be a symptom of insecurity or stress. Then again, it may be a bad habit. Once the child has been given a clean bill of health, he should be encouraged to adhere to the diet, within reason. Good, nourishing foods can be substituted for high-calorie goodies. An occasional fattening treat may be given at various times to give the dieter something to anticipate.

During the course of the diet program, be sure to give the child as much encouragement as possible. Alert friends, members of the family or other teachers, to pay the child a compliment now and then. Parents may be interested in providing a stimulus by agreeing to buy the child some new clothes. Boys and girls alike enjoy wearing the latest "fad" clothes, such as T-shirts decorated with pictures of a favorite hero, ball player or television star. If such an item were purchased too small to fit the child, it might offer an incentive for the child to get down to the size where it fits him. If it is something most of "the gang" is wearing, he will be eager to have it, too.

A program of exercise is worth considering. Most children attend physical education classes in school, and young children are generally active. Some, however, especially those who are overweight, have a tendency to choose inactive pastimes: watching television, playing cards or painting pictures. Make it a point to provide opportunities for the child to engage in activities that will burn up his extra calories.

Most children have not developed much self-control. It is therefore up to us to set an example and help them attain their goals. If we proceed with patience and understanding rather than impatience and criticism, we will help the child to his best advantage.

—————— RECOMMENDED READING

Bannatyne, Alexander. *Language, Reading and Learning Disabilities*. Springfield, Ill.: C.C. Thomas, 1971.

Bradfield, Robert H. *Behavior Modification of Learning Disabilities*. San Rafael, Cal.: Academic Therapy Publications, 1971.
Cawley, John F. *The Slow Learner and the Reading Problem*. Springfield, Ill.: C.C. Thomas, 1972.
Love, Harold D. *Parents Diagnose and Correct Reading Problems*. Springfield, Ill.: C.C. Thomas, 1970.
Marzollo, Jean. *Learning Through Play*. New York: Harper and Row, 1972.

chapter 5

Janet
(A PROBLEM OF PERMANENT ABNORMALITY)

In the preceding chapter, we met Gary who was too big for his age. His size put him at a disadvantage in a classroom composed of normal-sized children. Janet was at the same disadvantage, but she was too small for her age, and, unlike Gary, there was no chance that her size would change. She was a true midget.

Her parents, both normal in size, had sought medical attention early in Janet's life. Physical examinations and laboratory tests revealed that abnormalities in her pituitary gland and other vital functions would permanently retard her growth.

Janet experienced difficulties in most school areas. She had difficulty holding pencils or crayons. Her tiny hands tired easily, yet she refused my offers to diminish the amount of work expected of her. In fact, she tried to accomplish more than her classmates, and this inevitably led to a deep frustration.

It was obvious that Janet was also frustrated at home. Sometimes her parents were overly strict with her, demanding impossible behavior. This may have been their way of wishing that Janet was a normal child. At other times, they were overly lenient. When Janet needed discipline, she was either ignored or given a compliment. This may have reflected an obscure sense of guilt for having produced an "abnormal" child. Whatever the reasons, her parents were not consistent in the ways in which they handled Janet. Consequently, she rarely knew what to do.

Janet's mother refused to have any more children, afraid they might be like Janet. She and her husband had been assured that the probability was most unlikely, as there were no other instances of stunted growth on either side of the family. Yet, because of their fear, they allowed Janet to be an only child, even though they had originally wanted three or four children.

When I spoke to Janet's mother, I asked her what problems she thought would arise if Janet had normal-size brothers and sisters. Her answers were typical of the way she thought:

"They would be midgets. I don't want to grow a family of freaks!"

"Even if they were normal, they would have to put up with an abnormal sister and explain her to their friends."

"It's hard enough to see poor Janet's heart breaking when she comes into contact with normal kids. It would be worse if she had to live with them twenty-four hours a day."

Janet's tiny size was not the only abnormal thing about her. She had an unusual voice, high-pitched and reedy, like a shrill musical instrument. There was a nerve-shattering quality about it that annoyed most people. All she had to do was whine for a few moments, and most people would give in to her wishes, just to keep her quiet.

In addition to her whining, Janet talked a great deal in school. Her unpleasant voice bothered her classmates. When I tried to encourage her to whisper, she refused to try. At last, I referred her to the speech therapist.

The speech therapist examined her and decided that there must be something wrong with her vocal cords. No amount of practice seemed to affect her vocal pitch. Since it was impossible to control the pitch, we began a program to encourage her to control the sound volume. Most of our efforts failed. I learned that some people cannot whisper, no matter how hard they try, just as some cannot ever learn to whistle.

As a result of our inability to teach Janet to be more soft spoken, we attempted to direct her toward other activities besides talking. This, at first, seemed impossible, for she interrupted her classmates, called out answers for them and literally "stole the show." Sometimes her classmates appreciated her brightness, as when she helped them solve a difficult problem; other times they were annoyed by her voice, as when she whined. In that respect, Janet received a "double dose" of ambivalence, both at home and in school. Getting the children to accept Janet as a helper, a quiet helper, was thus a challenge.

In actuality, the children preferred to help Janet. During gym or other physical activities, they tried to avoid her, for she got underfoot like a capricious kitten. Encounters with children bumping into her caused numerous bruises on her body, which she accepted in good humor, evidence that she felt a strong need to belong to a group in spite of what happened to her.

Some of the children treated her like a baby doll, a cause of resentment on Janet's part. Once, when she wrote on the chalkboard, a child fetched a chair to make her taller. She pushed aside the chair and kicked the child in the shins. Another time, a larger child offered to hold her on his lap during a movie so she could see the screen. Janet preferred to stand in the aisle throughout the entire film rather than be treated like a baby.

The fact that a dependent Janet tried to be independent caused her to suffer emotionally. I considered sending her to a psychologist for evaluation at first, but then decided to help her change her attitudes.

After seeing the film, *Snow White and the Seven Dwarfs,* we discussed the plot. Someone asked if the old men would ever get big. The children were confused that the dwarfs were small despite the fact that their gray beards indicated they were of an advanced age. One child asked if Janet would someday be like them, a little old gray-haired lady. The comment caused laughter. Janet's reaction indicated how sensitive she was about her condition. She shouted all the bad words she knew, and then stomped out of the room.

During a discussion about future occupations, someone asked Janet if she wanted to be a midget in a circus when she "grew up." The child who asked would have given up a chance to fly to the moon if he could join a circus, so the remark was not meant as an insult. Janet, however, interpreted it as such, and proclaimed that she was not a freak.

After many futile attempts, we were able to discover her ambition. She wanted to be an airline stewardess. A classmate mentioned that a stewardess must be a certain height, adding that her sister had been too tall to be accepted by a leading airline. She feared that she would take after her sister, a fact that would make it impossible for her to realize her similar ambition.

Janet seemed to relate to a child with a problem of size, even though the size was in the opposite direction. At first I thought it would be good to have Janet and the tall girl become close friends and share their common problem. But, when Janet learned that the girl's alternate ambition was to become a nurse, she lost interest in the relationship.

In what way could I help Janet become self-reliant and independent? As she excelled in her studies, it was obviously her social life and her attitudes which needed readjustment. She had not succeeded as a helper in the classroom; yet there must, I felt, be some way in which she could be of service to the other children.

One day an opportunity arose while we were monitoring the children's oral reading by tape-recording their voices. The children took turns operating the recording equipment. They proved inept, and more than once erased an important tape. When it was Janet's turn to operate the recorder, we discovered that her little fingers turned the knobs with proficiency, and that her intelligence gave her a quick understanding of the mechanism.

Janet became our audio-director. She enjoyed the task, and became so intent on operating the tape recorder that she stopped her incessant talking. Because of her skill and ability with the recorder, the children produced outstanding programs. As time went by, Janet's job gave meaning to her life. She was able to feel wanted and appreciated, and much of the effect of her abnormality was minimized.

COMMENTS

A child who is smaller or weaker than other children, or constitutionally inferior to them, can create a problem for himself. Teachers can take advantage of positive aspects of the child's makeup by finding tasks that the child can perform with success.

Classmates should be encouraged to help, but not to the point of rendering the child helpless, or creating a feeling of inferiority. A give-and-take atmosphere should be sought, in which individual differences, as well as similarities, are considered.

For example, Janet had a desire to become an airline stewardess and felt an affinity to the girl who, in all probability, would likewise, because of size, be unable to attain her goal. Janet lost interest in the girl, however, when she discovered the girl had another ambition which she could not possibly achieve. Had the girl shared Janet's interest in the tape recorder, the situation might have been entirely different.

Parents, also, should be encouraged to change their attitudes, along with the attitudes of the affected child. Parents need to refrain from pitying the child or themselves. The more "normal" the child can be considered, the better it is for all concerned. When Janet's parents realized how effectively she handled the audio equipment, they were delighted. Their attitude toward Janet changed. They began to expect more of her, and in turn, she gave them more.

As such a child grows older, the problems may increase. Classmates, or brothers and sisters grow bigger, while the child remains small. However, a good, healthy attitude developed at an early age will help to maintain the proper perspective in later years. The essential factor is the development of confidence and self-reliance. By experiencing success in various tasks, Janet gradually developed faith in herself.

The above-mentioned comments are true of any permanent physical limitation. Some children have poor vision, others have faulty coordination. Volumes have been written about physically handicapped children. The key to helping any handicapped child is *practical activity*. Give the child something definite to do, something which you feel he is capable of doing. If it makes sense to the child, it will have meaning for him in more ways than "keeping him busy." It will become a springboard that will help the child move out toward other activities in the future.

Janet's problem demonstrates that many times a child in trouble can be helped by teachers and parents without profes-

sional psychological help. Common sense and an understanding
of child behavior often suffice.

—————— RECOMMENDED READING

Bernard, Harold W. *Child Development and Learning*. Boston:
Allyn and Bacon, 1973.
Kaplan, Solomon A. *Growth Disorders in Children and Adolescents*.
Springfield, Ill.: C.C. Thomas, 1964.
Sarason, Irwin G. et al. *Reinforcing Productive Classroom Behavior:
A Teachers' Guide to Behavior Modification*. New York: Behav-
ioral Publications, 1972.
Strain, Phillip S. et al. *Teaching Exceptional Children: Assessing
and Modifying Social Behavior*. New York: Academic Press, 1976.

chapter 6

Michael
(A PROBLEM OF DEVIANCE)

Michael had unusual interests for an eight-year-old boy. Most of the boys in my classroom romped around in jeans, T-shirts and gym shoes; they collected baseball cards, and enjoyed getting grubby hands from examining objects that aroused their curiosity. Michael was impeccably groomed when he reported for school, and at the end of the day there was not a wrinkle or smudge on his clothing. He wore pastel slacks with a side zipper, printed blouses, girls' sneakers, and concentrated his interests on dolls and sewing.

There was a certain swing to his hips as he walked which evoked comments from older boys in other classrooms. While I realize that outward manifestations of so-called "masculinity" and "femininity" are becoming less of a criterion by which to judge a person, the manner in which Michael seemed to imitate females began to worry me.

Whenever Michael went out of the classroom on his own, he used the girls' lavatory instead of the boys'. At first I thought he might be overly curious about girls and was merely peeking; most young children go through a phase when they need to see what the other sex is like.

During recess time, when all of the children go out at the same time, I noticed that Michael did not use the urinals with the other boys but, rather, retreated to a stall. This was not cause for suspicion at first: Many young children normally have several bowel movements during the course of a day, and that might have been Michael's reason for using a stall. I might have believed that Michael also was overly modest, as some boys are and did not wish the other boys to see his genitals, but an incident occurred which brought Michael's odd behavior into focus.

The school crossing guard discovered Michael with two older boys. They had found an unlocked automobile in the parking lot and Michael was modeling a pair of girl's frilly underpanties for the other boys. Ordinarily, such behavior might be considered mere "silliness", but, as Michael exhibited other signs that something was wrong with his sexual attitudes, I decided to have him interviewed by a psychologist.

Before a psychologist could test him, it was necessary to obtain his mother's approval. I made an appointment with her. When I asked her about Michael's interest in girls' things, she informed me that "Michael was not a rough boy" and wanted to know what was wrong with girls' things.

After being assured that Michael's interest was a bit unusual, she admitted that she preferred him to be feminine. I discovered that Michael lived in an all-female household, with his mother and three sisters. His parents were divorced; the father had no visitation rights. What's more, Michael's mother did not wish to talk about her ex-husband. From the way she spoke, she seemed to have a negative attitude toward men.

"My girls and I can get along without men!" she said. I noticed that she seemed to include Michael in her statement about "her girls."

When I asked her why he wore girls' clothing and preferred to use the girls' lavatory, I learned that he was a recipient of hand-me-downs for allegedly economic reasons. His mother's income was limited; his sisters' clothing was still good enough for him to wear, and "besides, he looks cute," she said proudly.

When I asked about his curiosity concerning girls, shown by his attempts to learn about them from going into their lavatory, she expressed surprise, commenting that he knew all about girls, that everything at home was free and open, and that nudity was not discouraged.

"I don't want my girls to grow up to be prudes," she said. "I'm a completely liberated person myself."

At first she would not agree to have the boy seen by a psychologist. Ultimately, however, she changed her mind. He

41

"became impossible" at home, using her hair spray, perfume and bubble bath, borrowing her handbag, and "messing up" her underthings in the bathroom. Just what the "messing up" involved she was reluctant to explain; her obvious embarrassment led me to believe that there were sexual implications.

After many interviews with the psychologist, it was discovered that Michael preferred to urinate by sitting down the way girls do. It was not simply exposure at home and imitation of the females he had seen during his early years at home. According to the psychologist, Michael preferred to be a girl.

It became apparent that Michael might be heading for difficulties in his adult sexual role. The psychologist felt that these might be the kinds of behavior that could lead to homosexual behavior later on. Even Michael's attitude toward the psychologist showed evidence of a tendency towards sexual deviance. Michael openly flirted with the psychologist the way little girls usually do.

The psychologist asked me to help him conduct an informal test. We began a classroom project in which the children were asked to classify pictures according to categories, such as *Pets, Clothing, Toys,* and so on. The children made little booklets, giving them whatever titles they wished. We obtained several old Sears Roebuck Catalogues from which to cut pictures that would fit the categories chosen by each child.

Michael entitled his booklet "Shoes" and did an excellent job of classifying shoes according to type, such as dress, sports, lounging, informal, and so on. However, the styles were not designed for boys. His book contained feminine styles. When Michael displayed it, several boys snickered. Although Michael explained that he was planning to give it to his mother as a gift, I noticed that the booklet remained in his desk long after Mother's Day. I also observed Michael looking through it from time to time with obvious enjoyment.

Upon the psychologist's request, I kept a record of Michael's behavior and noted signs of deviant behavior. One incident was especially suspicious. During Show and Tell, a little girl brought in a doll and wardrobe. There were other "dolls" in the classroom, both boy and girl models which we used for self-expression and role-playing activities. It was not unusual for a boy to "become" Little Red Riding Hood during an acting session. It was obvious that the boy generally knew he was merely playing a part. Michael, however, seemed obsessed by the girl dolls, and especially by the doll's clothing which had been brought in for the day.

He dressed and undressed the doll over and over again all day long. The girls began to complain that they had not been given a chance to play with it. What's more, at the end of the day, the girl who owned the doll could not find some of its clothing. A swimsuit and a pair of shoes were missing. We searched the room to no avail. At last I did what I usually do when I suspect that someone has "stolen" something. I asked all of the children to look into their desks just in case the items had been dropped in by mistake. At the same time I pretended to search my own desk drawers. This, I believed, would save face if anyone had taken the clothing and wished to return it unobtrusively.

Because of Michael's behavior, I suspected him. To my surprise, Andrea "found" the things and returned them to the owner. I reminded myself to be less suspicious of Michael in the future. It is a temptation to any child, seeing an attractive toy, to try to keep it. It is likewise easy for a teacher to fall into the trap of drawing conclusions too hastily. Because I had set myself to look for certain responses in Michael, I thought I would find them.

I kept a record of all unusual behavior in Michael, and discussed it with the psychologist. Eventually, he recommended psychiatric examination of the boy, for which Michael's mother's permission was required. At first she again refused to cooperate. In a moment of confidence, she related to me that she was afraid of what the "shrink," as she called him, would think about her, for she was made aware that parents as well as the child must undergo examination if the therapy is to be really effective. However, she ultimately agreed.

Psychiatric examination brought to light many interesting facts. Michael's mother disliked men in general and Michael's father in particular. Whenever Michael exhibited a trait that reminded her of his father, he was punished. This confused him because he could not understand what wrong he had done. Furthermore, his mother was always too enraged at the moment to explain the situation to him.

On the other hand, she rewarded him when he imitated his sisters. She did not stop to think about rewards and punishments as such, and how they could influence the boy's future behavior. Hers was an entirely emotional reaction, in which she allowed her bitter feelings toward men to rule her relationship with her son.

All traces of his father's belongings had been removed from their home. There was nothing "masculine" to inspire Michael to respond as a boy. He craved his mother's attention, and feared that she would reject him if he did not behave the way she wanted. Consequently, her approving gestures and remarks whenever he did something that pleased her acted as positive reinforcers. It was more pleasant for him to exhibit behavior which his mother would reward. Because his teachers were women, Michael was exposed to a similar situation in school.

The first step in Michael's therapy was a complete physical examination. The psychiatrist needed to know whether or not feminine goals were desirable for him. It was found that he was anatomically a complete male.

Every effort was made to re-orient Michael toward a male role in life. Some of the more liberated faculty members believed that he should have been given a chance to choose for himself. They cited sex-change surgical procedures as examples of "liberation."

Nevertheless, it was decided that Michael was too young at that point in his life to determine intelligently and objectively the sex role that he truly wanted or needed. By showing him possible alternatives and by encouraging him to try the role that society expected of him, it was felt that he had a better chance for happiness when he matured. If, despite the opportunity to learn new behavior, he persisted in wishing to be a female, then the picture would change.

Some of the role-strengthening activities we employed were as follows:

1. Michael was given the opportunity to spend part of each day, every day, with men. Sometimes it was the psychologist, the psychiatrist, guidance counselor, boys' gym teacher, shop instructor or the school crossing guard. At home, Michael's mother began to help by

44

inviting his uncle to participate in social events. She bought tickets to athletic games for Michael and his uncle to attend together. This was difficult for her, because the uncle was her ex-husband's brother and had many mannerisms of her ex-husband. She made the effort to tolerate him for Michael's sake.

2. Michael's mother underwent therapy herself. She began to realize that her attitudes were affecting her son in a harmful way. She tried to overcome her hatred of "crude" activities, such as football and wrestling. She allowed Michael to watch those events on television, although she could not bring herself to attend any such events personally. She did join a group of people who were interested in bowling, and eventually began to enjoy Saturday afternoons bowling with Michael and his sisters and friends. In addition, she met some friends of her own, some of whom were men, and she began to realize that being masculine was not undersirable for Michael.

3. Michael stopped taking music lessons, which he hated, and which his mother had forced him to take. His competence in playing the flute had encouraged his mother to believe that he could help her realize her life-long dream—to be an accompanist to a handsome male soloist. As she was an expert pianist, that dream had seemed possible if her son would eventually become the soloist. Instead of music lessons, Michael joined the Cub Scouts. His interest in music was kept alive by encouragement to become the scouts' bugler at camp.

Being the bugler helped him to relate to the other ac-activities at the Scout camp. Although at first he felt out of place with boys his own age, the Scout leader, a sympathetic, understanding man, helped in many ways: He took him shopping for his uniform and equipment; he suggested that Michael's sisters become Girl Scouts. After a while, Michael began to compare notes with his sisters about the various activities in their respective camps, and some healthy male-female competition ensued.

4. Michael's mother overcame her need to keep the house

excessively neat. She bought a dog for the children, a male collie that she wanted to name "Prince." Michael exhibited his first real independence by insisting that the dog be named "Guts."

5. At school, Michael was placed in groups which contained as many boys as girls. Sometimes he preferred to work with a girl, other times he chose a boy. I noticed that his preference began to depend upon competence rather than sex. The fact that he was able to choose someone on the basis of qualification showed that he was able to make judgments on an intellectual instead of an emotional level. This was in his favor, proving that he was responding to help. Ultimately, as his distress signals were detected and diagnosed, Michael's problem disappeared.

--- COMMENTS

If Michael's problem had not been detected early enough, he might have run into serious troubles later in life. As in all cases of problem children, early detection is one of the most important aspects of helping the child. In giving you the details of Michael's problem, I hope you may get some insight into similar problems that you may encounter.

Children of either sex can and should be encouraged to explore as many facets of human behavior as possible. Books, toys and other articles used by children should be assigned to neither sex. It is natural for children to be interested in everything. Modern educators encourage boys to play with what were formerly considered "girls' toys," such as baby dolls, and girls to try out "boys' things," such as football helmets. This satisfies the children's curiosity, prepares them for the future by exposing them to many stimuli, and ultimately enables them to choose interests freely and without bias.

The school in which I teach has recently instituted courses in Shop for girls. They learn to use tools, repair electrical appliances and operate machines. Similarly, boys are given a course in Home Economics, and they learn to cook, plan meals, care for small children and sew. The courses are made meaningful by the fact that the girls construct a small cabinet for their cosmetics, and the boys sew heavy carpenters' aprons for use in a workshop. Since such activities are interesting and important to people of both sexes, the program has become quite successful.

Again, moderation and avoidance of extremes in dealing with sex equality is desirable. For example, some schools do not separate boys' and girls' lavatories. Recent incidents in hospitals and other institutions that allowed "coeducational" lavatory facilities have led us to believe that a certain amount of privacy, if not modesty, is required for the safety and well-being of most individuals.

Teachers and parents play an important role in a child's attitude toward his sexual role. If, for instance, a boy seems to choose to be "feminine," it may be well to direct his interests discreetly toward "masculine" aspects of life. In this context, "masculine" and "feminine" are used in a strictly sexual, biological sense.

Modern books for youngsters contain stories in which there are female truck drivers and male nurses. Equal opportunity is given to persons regardless of sex. However, I feel that mother and father roles are still prevalent in our society and should therefore be perpetuated. It is desirable that the roles be sharply defined so that the child can imitate one or the other without confusion. Young children need both a strong father image and a healthy mother attachment.

Let us consider children from "inner city" or "disadvantaged" homes, which are often one-parent homes. Fatherless children profit greatly from experience with a male teacher who offers to boys and girls alike the necessary father-figure. Then again, children with working mothers, who have not had the opportunity of being "mothered" at home, will respond favorably in most instances to a female teacher.

We are going through a revolution of sexual change in our society, but one question should be kept in mind: What will the social values be when the children in our care become adults? We can only imagine the answer. But because the purpose of true education is to prepare children to be responsible, well-adjusted adults, we who educate children should at least help them to play a healthy biological role in any future society.

All children go through phases during which they are attracted to people of the same sex. This is perfectly normal and should not be discouraged. Only when, as in Michael's case, the behavior points toward deviation from the accepted behavior should we make an effort to intervene.

—————— RECOMMENDED READING

Feldman, Maurice P. and M.J. MacCulloch. *Homosexual Behavior.* New York: Pergamon Books, 1971.

Lamb, Michael E. *The Role of the Father in Child Development.* New York: Wiley, 1976.

Ollendorff, Robert H. *The Juvenile Homosexual Experience and Its Effect on Adult Sexuality.* New York: Julian Press, 1966.

Plummer, Kenneth. *Sexual Stigma.* (Including Bibliographical Index). Boston: Routledge & Kegan Paul, 1975.

Porteous, Hedy S. *Sex and Identity: Your Child's Identity.* Indianapolis: Bobbs-Merrill, 1972.

Rosenberg, Benjamin George. *Sex and Identity.* New York: Holt, Rinehart & Winston, 1972.

Weinberg, Martin S. *Homosexuality: An Annotated Bibliography.* New York: Harper & Row, 1972.

Wyden, Peter and Barbara. *Growing Up Straight.* New York: Stein and Day, 1968.

chapter 7

Frances
(A PROBLEM OF APPARENT DEVIANCE)

Like Michael in the previous chapter, Frances took a marked interest in things belonging to the opposite sex. She enjoyed wearing boys' clothing, including their sneakers. I often observed her stepping into a puddle to get her feet wet, which made it necessary for her to borrow a classmate's shoes. Invariably, despite the fact that her feet were small enough to wear a girl's size, she insisted that none of the girls' gym shoes fit. The fact of the matter was that Frances liked wearing boys' sneakers.

At our school, boys and girls in third grade participated in physical education classes together. The gym teacher informed me that Frances refused to participate in rhythmic activities such as folk dancing, which she considered "silly," preferring more strenuous activities, such as climbing ropes, push-ups and tumbling.

She did not answer to her own name. We had to call her "Frank" before we got her attention. I did not know if she was being stubborn on purpose, or whether she was so accustomed to the nickname at home that she did not hear any other name.

"Frank" was a true tomboy, frequently getting into fights with boys. Indeed, she usually instigated the fights by declaring that she could beat up anybody who dared to take her on. Of course this was a great challenge to the boys. Whenever a new boy joined the school, "Frank" dared him to "lick" her. She proved to be faster, tougher, and more cunning than any of the boys, none of whom ever won in a fight with her.

She did not associate with other girls. They did not like her rough ways. In this sense, Frances had no real friends among her classmates, and appeared to be a lonely little girl behind a facade of exterior toughness.

Actually, the children seemed to be afraid of her. At our Halloween party, for example, she won the prize for "best costume." The children themselves awarded her the prize, which surprised me until I learned that she had threatened to beat up anyone who failed to vote for her. When she selected her prize, she took the boy's item, a miniature sports car. When the boys wanted to examine it, she made a fist at them, so they stayed away.

"Frank" liked football and expressed a desire to become a football player when she grew up. In a general discussion we talked about realistic goals, stressing the fact that football teams were generally composed of men, and that women usually played touch football rather than the tackle variety.

When she realized that her chances of becoming a real men's quarterback were small, she decided to become a fireman or garbageman. She adored collecting trash that was left outside in cans on collection days. Her idea of a fascinating Show and Tell was more often Show and *Smell*.

"Frank's" behavior in class was often disruptive. In addition to picking fights, she hit other children while they tried to work, or threw things at them. I saw her more than once stick her foot in the aisle and purposely trip a child. In pleasant weather, she tossed paper airplanes out the window. She chewed chocolate caramels, spitting the juice in imitation of a tobacco-chewing man. Occasionally, she snipped off some hair with classroom scissors. It was usually her own hair, when it became too long to suit her, but sometimes that of a boy.

As her behavior seemed to be a signal of distress, I decided to consult a psychologist. The psychologist discovered that "Frank's" family background was similar to Michael's, in the sense that she was the only girl in what was practically an all-male household. There was a mother, but she worked all day in a factory as a machinist, and on her days off, she took the children—three boys and "Frank"—on motorcycle outings. Her boyfriend, who generally accompanied them, had very masculine interests such as racing cars, hunting and hang gliding.

The mother was divorced and she did not want her three sons to grow up without the companionship of an adult male. If her boyfriend was not available for that purpose, she herself played the role of "buddy" to the boys. Frances emulated her mother and brothers. She found it was a good thing to act like the boys, as that was the best way to compete for her mother's attention and meet with the approval of her brothers at the same time.

The psychologist felt that Frances was a victim of home exposure. As his caseload was too large for him to handle Frances immediately, we decided to try to help the child in the classroom before attempting to change anything in her home environment.

It was important that we not go to extremes as her mother had. By trying to be both mother and father to the children, the mother had actually been neither. What Frances needed was some feminine companionship to round out her personality.

She had to learn to function without being overly rough. She needed to unclench her fists and learn to shake hands. We did not want her to stop enjoying the activities she liked, but wanted her to learn to know other kinds of activities and add them to her list of accomplishments. This would enable her to get along with other children and eventually help her to acquire some friends.

A teacher in another classroom became irate when Frances beat up one of the boys in his room, and suggested letting "that darn girl" get beat up herself, just to see how it felt to meet her match. This "eye-for-an-eye" philosophy did not appeal to me. I was convinced that it would not make Frances any better, and I further felt that it might even make her more eager to retaliate.

I needed a first step for the girl. In such cases, it is sometimes difficult to know where to begin. Because I knew that she would not accept hints or suggestions, I decided to give her an order, a direct command to do something, even though I was aware that she would dislike doing it.

The teachers were planning a tea party to celebrate teachers' recognition day. Girls from various classrooms were being asked to help. Their jobs ranged from pouring tea to arranging flowers for the tables. The idea of a tea party was the most ridiculously "feminine" activity I could imagine.

I called Frances aside and told her it was her turn to be a hostess. The face she made was a study in disbelief.

"You gotta be kiddin'!" she retorted.

"Look, *Frances*," I said, emphasizing her correct name, "it's about time you did something useful around this school!" Then I added, "I don't suppose you're afraid to boil water for tea, are you? You might spill some and get burned."

"I'm not afraid of anything," she announced.

"Perhaps you are," I said. It was a verbal dare. I was "putting up my fists" and she seemed to sense a fight approaching. It was not her nature to back down from a good fight, so she accepted the challenge.

I could have told her that anybody could pour tea, and that it took a special person to boil the water. This might have worked with another child, but Frances was too intelligent to accept such obvious flattery, and too much of a rebel to comply or conform.

On the day of the tea, Frances arrived at school wearing jeans and her leather jacket, while the other girls wore pantsuits or dresses. I introduced her as *Frances*. She seemed embarrassed at first, then resentful. For about a half hour she stood at the stove in the kitchen. Then she disappeared, leaving one of the teakettles boiling until someone else took her place.

When I learned that she had left, I became alarmed. It had been a risky business in the first place. Perhaps I had no right to challenge her in that way. I had felt that I was speaking her language by providing her with a chance to fight back in the only way she knew. Evidently she had been unable to prove herself in this situation and had run away from it. If that were the case, more wrong had been done than right.

I left the party and found Frances in the parking lot, going from car to car and kicking the tires in a gesture of defiance. There was a slump to her shoulders that suggested defeat. When I called to her—*Frances*, for I did not want her to think she had won this issue which she might do if I reverted to *Frank*—she did not respond. She looked toward me out of the corner of her eye, though, so I knew she heard her name.

When I caught up to her, I said, "They're running out of hot water."

"So what? Big deal! Anybody can boil dumb water! How come I got the stupidest job?" she asked.

"Do you really want to know?" I asked in return. She

52

looked surprised. "You mean I got that job for a reason?" she asked, her eyes popping open in surprise.

"In a way, you asked for it," I said.

"How?"

"Well, now, how would it look for you to put on an apron and serve pretty little cookies like the rest of the ladies at the party?"

"Dumb," she answered, averting her eyes.

"Have you ever poured tea?" I asked.

"No, but what's the big deal about doing a dumb thing like that?" she wanted to know.

"It's one of the social graces," I said, "like dancing, playing tennis, or whatever. The more things you know how to do— and do properly—the better chances you have of being popular. Then people want to include you in their activities. So what if you don't go to teas every day—it's nice to know how to act at one when you get an invitation."

Her face became serious. "I never want to go to another dumb tea as long as I live!" she said.

"Who knows? If you can act properly at a tea, then you may also act nicely at any kind of party. People will sense that you're a good person to have around. They'll invite you to other affairs. Don't you like getting invitations?"

"No one ever invites me anywhere. Besides, my family is busy. We do everything together. We have a lot of fun."

"I'm sure you do," I answered. "Has it ever occurred to you that your mother may also like to entertain her friends— with parties such as this one today? Perhaps she doesn't dare."

"Why not?"

"Because she's afraid she might bore the boys with sissy stuff."

"My mother can make tea!" said Frances indignantly.

"That's the point. I'm sure she can do just about anything. So can you. Why do you have to do just certain things—for instance, fight with boys?"

She looked at me for a long interval. At last she admitted that she did not mean to fight. We talked for some time, and she confided that she had never talked with her mother as she talked to me. We agreed that she would try again to help at some social affair.

53

During our next "girl-to-girl" talk, we discussed other occasions which were planned at school. She agreed to accept a job as hostess, writing name tags on gummed labels, at the next social gathering.

With some misgivings, she showed up for the party wearing a new pantsuit and girls' shoes. Despite the fact that she said she felt silly, there was a determined look in her eye. Her job gave her adequate opportunity to observe how others behaved. Afterward, I asked her how she had felt.

"I still think it's silly," she said, adding, "The Home Ec teacher complimented me on my good printing. She asked if I'd make place cards for the graduation dinner next month. In fact, she needs some help with the table decorations."

"Are you going to accept?" I asked.

"I already said I would," she said.

Because she was on the decorating committee, Frances was allowed to remain for the festivities following the graduation dinner. There was dancing and fun, and she saw boys and girls getting along together without fighting.

By that time, she had become interested in other activities besides sports. She helped paint scenery for a school play. It was a cooperative effort, not a competitive one. Eventually, Frances began to develop into a fairly well-rounded person.

Her mother helped, too. When she became aware of the problem, she planned activities for Frances' benefit. Frances began taking interpretive dancing lessons in a class of boys and girls which gave her freedom to exert her physical prowess. She began to study music and decided upon the drum as her instrument. Most of this happened after she left my classroom. I followed her school career and discovered that she played bass drum in her high school marching band, preferring it to being a cheerleader. Her choice was a realistic goal.

COMMENTS

Frances' case shows what can happen if behavior is carried to an extreme. Her mother overreacted to her divorce by trying to be both parents to her children, in the belief that her boys needed male attention. That was true, of course, but what she forgot was the fact that she also had a little girl who needed a mother's attention. Frances needed to identify with a responsible female adult in order to grow into a socially acceptable woman.

Teachers and guardians alike should be warned about making generalizations. It may have been a temptation to put Frances in a category similar to Michael's, and thus suspect her of sexual deviation. In Frances' case, however, sexual deviance was not the problem, as time and patience demonstrated. Frances craved feminine attention, and when she felt understood, her aggressive behavior was channeled into acceptable activities.

She was given books about female Olympic champions whom she could emulate. She became an enthusiastic tennis player and swimmer. In this age of sedentary habits, we should keep in mind the importance of encouraging physical activity, which is prerequisite to a good, all-around healthy personality in any field of endeavor.

Some children will not respond to the direct way in which I challenged Frances. The fact that I met her at her own level was important, for she was accustomed to meeting physical challenges. I substituted another type of challenge which she accepted. Meeting the child at his or her level is not lowering standards as some teachers believe, but rather the basis of true communication. If the child cannot understand you, then you must make an effort to reach the child in whatever way you can. Sometimes spending as much time as possible with the child will help you learn what avenues are open. In this way you can get to know the child's feelings, strengths, weaknesses and preferences.

The signal that Frances sent out was perplexing. She disrupted her classmates, and confused the issue by seeming to want to be a boy. All she was really doing, however, was behaving the way she had learned to do at home. For this reason, it is advisable for teachers and parents to work together. The child, after all, brings the home situation to school, and frequently takes the school situation home.

It is encouraging to realize that Frances was helped without formal psychological counseling. Many children can be helped by teachers and parents who know something of the basic needs of human beings. We all need to be wanted, and to feel accepted. We need the approval of others, especially our peers. By studying the aspects of Frances' case, you may see how some of those needs were met.

——— RECOMMENDED READING

Harrison, Barbara G. *Unlearning the Lie: Sexism in School*. New York: Liveright, 1973.

Lynn, David Brandon. *Parental and Sex-Role Identification*. Berkeley, Cal.: McCutchan Publishing Corp., 1969.

Smith, Brian S. and Benjamin G. Rosenberg. *Sex and Identity*. New York: Holt, Rinehart & Winston, 1972.

Yorburg, Betty. *Sexual Identity—Sex Roles and Social* Change. New York: Wiley, 1974.

chapter 8

Carl

(A PROBLEM OF PSYCHOLOGICAL TRAUMA)

The moment Carl's mother learned that our school was to be integrated, she came to see me, requesting that Carl be placed in a classroom containing only white children.

"Carl will get sick if he has to be in the same room with black kids," she said. It was apparent that she was upset beyond the point of most of the other white parents, whose prejudices had created feelings of misgivings about the integration program. Some had quietly enrolled their children in private schools; others had decided to give the program a chance, but none had reacted as strongly as Carl's mother.

When I informed her that each classroom would contain children of all racial backgrounds, she became more upset. Until then, she had been satisfied with our school, even though Carl had not progressed as well as most other children.

Carl's first few weeks in kindergarten had been a "nightmare" for the teacher. Carl would not stay in the room unless his mother was there. At first the teacher allowed his mother to stay in order to put Carl at his ease. However, the moment he noticed that she had left even momentarily, he burst into fits of hysterical crying and did not stop until she returned.

After a great deal of time and effort, it became possible for Carl's mother to stay out of his sight. She remained in the corridor or the school office, however, just in case Carl needed her. Little by little Carl became accustomed to her absence, and by the end of the year he was able to get along without her. However, she continued to drive him to school every day and to pick him up when school was dismissed.

It was thought best for him to experience another year in kindergarten, as he had not learned the basic skills needed for first grade, such as dressing himself, tying his shoelaces and finding his own way home. In his second year he made only a slight improvement and the teacher believed that he was a victim of an overly protective mother.

His year in first grade was even more dismal. He was absent a good deal because of illnesses which his mother called "upset stomach" or "intestinal flu". Because he missed so much basic work, the first grade teacher decided to have him repeat the grade. While most mothers dislike having a child "fail," Carl's mother seemed glad that he would remain with younger children.

The subsequent year in first grade, and one full year in second grade, allowed him to catch up in his work.

By the time he reached my third grade, he was a fairly good student. Although he was almost 10, he was small for his age and thus blended in with the younger children.

Because Carl was doing well in school at last, I felt that his mother's plans to transfer him to a private school would do him more harm than good. It was obvious that Carl had trouble adjusting to new situations. When I mentioned this to his mother, she replied, "You don't understand."

When I asked her why she thought Carl would become ill if placed in a classroom with black children, she reluctantly told me that he had witnessed the rape of his teen-age sister by a black man. Carl, only four at the time, had been walking home from a store with his sister at twilight. A black man jumped out of some bushes and attacked her. She fought with him, bruising her head as she fell against a mailbox post.

Carl was so frightened by the unexpected attack that he had been unable to run or call for help. A passer-by noticed the young woman lying there, with a little boy beside her on the grass, rocking back and forth in a state of shock.

The family's reaction did little to help Carl overcome the shock. They refused to cooperate with the police in locating the rapist, for they were afraid the publicity would do more damage to the girl. One of the reasons they never discussed the incident was to protect the girl's reputation. It was imperative that no one at the school learn about the family's trouble, and consequently Carl's teachers had no way of knowing that this was the reason his mother "babied" him to the extent that she did.

Further, the family's attitude toward blacks became one of intolerance. If black persons were on the television screen, the set was immediately switched to another channel. Carl heard his parents make frequent derogatory remarks about "niggers."

After five years of such a background, Carl could not stand the sight of blacks, especially black men. He shook with fear at the sight of them, and sometimes developed severe headaches or attacks of violent vomiting.

I liked Carl and wanted to help him. He enjoyed school and seemed to like me. To cause him to leave his present situation in order to escape from an umpleasant experience seemed unfair to him. I felt that he would have to face integration sooner or later in the course of his academic life and that acceptance of it and black people would benefit him in every phase of his life. Consequently, I asked his mother to allow him the chance to see that all black people were not the same, and that the man who hurt his sister was not typical of the race.

With some misgivings, Carl's mother agreed to allow him to remain in the school. She warned me, though, that she would remove him immediately at the first sign of trouble.

On the day of the black children's arrival, I made sure that none of them was seated near Carl. This took a bit of juggling, as I wanted to scatter the children about the room so they would not be isolated into a subgroup of their own, a circumstance that might call attention to their difference. On the other hand, to make them feel more at ease among strangers, I wanted to be sure that at least two of them were close enough to each other to talk or otherwise communicate.

Although Carl's work was sketchy that day, he did not become ill. He claimed that his hand was sore from playing ball, causing his writing to be careless. For his sake, I accepted his story, even though I suspected that his hand was shaking as a result of his emotional reaction to the black children.

For milk-break each morning, children took turns bringing cookies. When a black child offered Carl a cookie, he consistently refused to accept it, even though he took cookies from

Oriental or Indian children. He never said anything rude to the black children, which I considered good self-control on his part, but tended to stay out of their way.

As the black children were accepted by the class as a whole, I hoped they would interpret Carl's aloofness as shyness. All the while, I looked for a way to help prove to Carl that most blacks were not as he thought, and that he could profit by having some black children for friends. To force such a responsibility upon him too quickly would have proved disastrous. I was grateful that he had not responded as his mother had feared he would and decided to let the situation slide along until an opportunity to make my point presented itself.

It became Sharon's turn to bring cookies. She was one of the new black children, a sweet child with an outgoing personality. Because I knew she could not afford cookies, I bought some of Carl's favorites. At milk-break time, I handed them to Sharon and asked her to pass them to the children.

She paused at Carl's desk and offered him one of the lovely pink cookies. In my mind's eye, I envisioned him standing suddenly and tossing the tray of cookies to the floor. Perhaps he would scream at Sharon, run out of the room, or become violently ill. This was the first time any of the black children had paused at his side after seeing him shake his head. When she continued to stand there, it was obvious that he had to do something. She commented that they were delicious and gave him a friendly smile. He looked at her, licked his lips, and then his hand reached for and took a cookie. She immediately went to the next child. There were enough cookies for a second time around. Carl did not hesitate to accept a cookie from her when she approached him again.

After that it was not a case of miraculous recovery for Carl. He still refused cookies from other black children. However, the fact that he *did* respond favorably to Sharon proved that he was capable of relating to a black individual on a one-to-one basis. Before that, he had been making generalizations about the race as a whole.

After several months and many rearrangements of the desks, Carl was seated next to David, a black boy. Although Carl and David did not become close friends as seatmates often do, they did not fight or otherwise display antagonism to each other. On the contrary, Carl occasionally chose David as a partner in games. He did it, I suspect, more out of his sense of fair play than friendship. At least it showed that Carl was beginning to overcome his prejudice and fear.

COMMENTS

A shocking psychological episode can, and does, leave scars. Parents' attitudes toward such an episode can add to the problem. A four-year-old who witnesses a frightening scene is shocked enough, without subsequently seeing and hearing the upsetting reactions of distraught parents.

It was certainly natural for Carl's parents to be upset by the rape of their daughter. Undoubtedly they felt justified in reacting as they did. Few people are prepared for such violence.

Many children are exposed to situations far less shocking than rape. Yet, they become just as upset as Carl, mainly because of the reaction of the adults in their environment.

I chose to tell about Carl's case because it was extreme. Rape is a nasty crime, terrible enough for adults to witness while standing by helplessly, as exemplified in cases where a criminal rapes a man's wife and the man is forced to watch the assault. But, at least the man understands the sexual process and, as incensed as he is by the crime, it is within the realm of his experience.

Consider, by contrast, a small boy who knows nothing of the sexual act and who witnesses the sister he loves being brutalized in a completely inexplicable way.

It is one matter to answer a small child's question, "Where do babies come from?" and touch upon the rudiments of human anatomy and physiology; it is another matter entirely to find the right words to answer when a child puts such questions as, "What did the policeman mean by the word *rape?*" or "Where did all the blood come from?" or, perhaps, "What did the man use to hurt my sister?"

I suspect that Carl's parents were afraid they would be confronted by such questions and were at a loss to know how to answer. Such questions are difficult to explain directly, especially when the person asked is in a state of anxiety over the experience. The very fact that anxiety exists tells the inquiring child a great deal about the emotional nature of the incident, much more than words alone could convey. As difficult as it may seem, the wise parent should at least try to keep cool-headed over such an occurrence, especially if being observed by a small child.

The opposite extreme, of course, is treating the occurrence as if it is of no consequence. This, too, should be avoided whenever possible. Failure even to mention the event may raise serious questions in a young child's mind. If it is dropped immediately, while it is still fresh in the child's consciousness, the child may become anxious. This may be caused by nothing more than mere curiosity, or it may be a result of genuine shock.

Fortunately, most children forget easily and live in the present. A child should be engaged in happy activities as soon as possible after such an emotional jolt. If enough joyous atmosphere surrounds the child, it is to be hoped that he will become enveloped in it, and that, little by little, the unpleasantness will grow dim.

Carl's parents kept the unpleasantness always in mind. They refused to watch black people on television; they made prejudiced comments, and they overprotected Carl, thereby imposing an awful burden upon him.

It is wise for a teacher to look into a child's background for a picture of his total emotional climate. If flare-ups occur, they can be put into perspective when their cause is known. In Carl's case, his teachers did not know why his mother treated him as she did, and thus they considered his behavior "immature."

When the reason for Carl's mother's attitude was at last known, it was possible for Carl to be helped. However, it took time. For example, Carl could not be rushed into accepting black children, and he was not forced to sit beside them right away. No issue was made over his refusal to accept cookies from them at first. If I had focused attention on his immediate reaction, it might have caused him to keep his negative attitudes. Chances are his school work would have continued to suffer as the years went by. His unhappiness might have caused his mother to transfer him to another school, thus teaching him to run away from unpleasant situations.

A child is not equipped to face difficult emotional situations head on, but should be shown, through gentle persuasion and positive encouragement how to handle them. All the while, the child should be treated as a child. By this, I do not mean he should be "babied," but rather that he be expected to accept only what it is within a young child's ability to grasp.

Teachers and parents who let their emotions run away with them, or who become overly anxious and upset in the presence of a child, do not set a good example. Adult self-control eventually won Carl over. With time, he was able to overcome some of the fear and prejudice he had observed in his parents. They, too, by seeing his improvement, felt more optimistic about the future.

It is unrealistic to maintain that we have no prejudices of one kind or another. What we should keep in mind is that our prejudices are generally transferred to our children and may limit their acceptance of the world they live in. Teachers as well as parents should try to be as open minded as possible. They will be rewarded by better communication with the children in their care, and the children will benefit greatly from having an unwarped view of their world.

———— # RECOMMENDED READING

Brown, Alan R. *Prejudice in Children*. Springfield, Ill.: Thomas Co., 1972.

Goodman, Mary Ellen. *Race Awareness in Young Children*. New York: Collier Books, 1964.

Jones, James M. *Prejudice and Racism*. Reading, Mass.: Addison-Wesley Publishing Co., 1972.

Mack, Raymond W. *Prejudice and Race Relations*. Chicago: Quadrangle Books, 1970.

chapter 9

Holly
(A PROBLEM OF STRESS)

On the first day of school, Holly carried a box of tissues, a dampened face cloth, and a towel to keep in her desk. Her mother explained that Holly suffered from nosebleeds and these had created some anxious moments in the second grade classroom the previous year.

Holly's mother assured me, however, that Holly would never hemorrhage, because the condition was not physical, but rather emotional, "due to Holly's nerves." Whenever the child became upset, her nose began to bleed. If the bleeding did not stop within a reasonable time, I was to telephone her mother, who would come to school immediately. Meanwhile, Holly knew exactly what to do in the event of a nosebleed.

Just to be on the safe side, our school doctor examined Holly and telephoned her physician. It was confirmed that Holly had no hemorrhagic disease. The doctor who had been treating Holly since infancy stated that she was a sensitive child, subject to anxiety if placed under too much pressure. As her stress threshold was low, I was warned to avoid putting her in any situation that might create tension and worry. This was particularly true in regard to competition with other children.

Holly was absent several times during the first weeks of school. The reason was always the same; nosebleeds. She recovered sufficiently to attend school in the afternoon upon those occasions. As it is my custom to schedule a "fun activity" late in the day to avoid boredom and motivate the children for the next day's lessons, I suspected that Holly did not want to miss the afternoon activities.

I decided to try a fun activity in the morning. In December, just before the Christmas vacation, a half day of school was scheduled. Because Holly's birthday occurred during the recess interval, I asked her if she would like to have her birthday party on that morning. She said she would and a party was arranged. As with all party days, excitement ran high. Holly brought some cupcakes and napkins, wore a special hat, and sat in the throne chair reserved for birthday children. Her cheeks were flushed and she spoke with animation, excitement which could precipitate a bleeding attack. However, she got through the morning nicely.

I decided that she had been prepared for the routine by having participated in other parties and thus knowing exactly what was expected of the birthday child. What's more, she had brought in the refreshments ahead of time, and felt secure that her party would be a success.

Because this technique worked well, I gave Holly the opportunity to take trial tests. These tests were made up of the same questions that would appear on the actual tests and thus gave Holly, as well as the other children, confidence that they would be successful. As a motivation, I allowed children who answered all of the trial test questions accurately to be exempt from the actual test. As Holly enjoyed painting at the easel, she tried to get the trial test questions right, so that she would have an opportunity to paint during testing time. The prospect was so pleasant that she did not seem to regard the trials as a challenge, for she knew that she always had another chance.

In the spring we had an assembly program about art. An easel was to be set up on the stage, beside which there would be a bucket of red paint and a large brush. Various children would draw lines, circles and squares with the brush. Other children would add to these basic forms to create various objects. The culmination of the act was to be a quick painting of Mickey Mouse's head.

During the painting of Mickey Mouse, we planned to play the record of the Mickey Mouse Club Marching Song. When I timed the music, I discovered that it took 58 seconds, meaning that the artist chosen to paint the mouse head had to do it in less than a minute.

All of the children practiced painting the mouse. We made no attempt to time the work. In fact, I did not mention how fast the painting had to be done. At that point, the important factor was painting a resembalance to the character of Mickey Mouse. It was with mixed emotions that I learned that the children themselves voted Holly to do the painting.

To ask her to paint a picture in record time before an audience would obviously put her under strain. She would want to create a good finale for the show, but I did not want her to do so at the expense of getting a nosebleed in the process.

One way to solve the problem was to prepare Holly in advance for the experience, as she had been prepared for her party and for the tests. I made several pencil sketches of the mouse, starting with two large circles for ears and numbered the other parts in sequence. This enabled Holly to work in an orderly, methodical fashion. Because she enjoyed painting, she had fun and felt no anxiety or tension. I let her go ahead in her own style at first. Then I suggested that she hold the brush more *boldly,* purposely avoiding the words *quickly* or *fast.* I encouraged her to apply more paint to the brush and to sweep it across the paper with broad strokes.

We put a canvas drop cloth on the floor so she did not have to worry about spills and spatters. Her hand and arm became relaxed. Day after day she painted with more abandon, her hand moved freely and, without realizing it, she began to finish the portraits rapidly.

When I knew she was not aware of me, I timed her work. One day I noted that she was able to complete the picture in less than the required time.

The following day we played music while the children painted. In this way, the singers could practice their parts, too. Eventually we played the Mickey Mouse Club March. When Holly finished the portrait before the march ended, the children applauded. She was amazed at her accomplishment and because she knew she was able to perform in front of an audience, consisting of her classmates on this occasion, she did not worry about the program.

To maintain her confidence, Holly was encouraged to perform the same task many times. Each time, she gained speed without realizing it. Just in case something unexpected happened during the actual performance in the auditorium, I wanted to allow for recovery time, so I asked Holly to wait for a musical cue before putting on the finishing touches.

66

Holly now believed that she was actually working too fast for the music. Because she regarded the music as something that possessed precision timing, something that she could depend on time and again, she felt no anxiety about competing with it, for she knew just where she stood.

On the day of the performance Holly was perfect. It seemed just like another trial run for her. All of the children enjoyed their parts as much as she did. There was not the usual last-minute stage fright because everyone was well prepared.

Because we had decided to keep the nature of Holly's part a secret, her mother was amazed to learn that Holly could perform under such conditions. Others in the audience commented on the unique, beat-the-record type of show. What they did not realize was that the act had become natural and routine because the children had previously experienced success and they were certain they would succeed again.

After the program, I talked with Holly's mother about the way we had dealt with her problem. Her mother decided to try similar routines at home. No attempt was made to change Holly's nature. She would probably always be a tense person, but now we knew some effective ways to deal with that tension.

COMMENTS

Most children are often under some form of stress or tension. It can be either physical or emotional in nature. Some actually need tension as a stimulus to learning, while others find tension difficult to overcome.

Some children become so tense during a test that they do not perform as well as they could. Many teachers give surprise tests, which prove nothing except that some children have prepared themselves in advance for a test. No child should ever be evaluated on the basis of such a test.

Educators generally agree that children should be prepared for tests. Some feel that tests should be eliminated altogether. However, we are educating large numbers of students and it is necessary to have some tangible basis for evaluation. The test situation also often helps a child prepare for later competition in his chosen vocational field. However, a person should never be judged on the basis of one test alone.

If you were to go to a doctor for a blood sugar test, for example, and you forgot to skip breakfast, the test would be inaccurate. If you ate several candy bars before the test, the resulting elevated blood sugar levels would be misleading. A doctor who finds a suspicious test result has the test repeated under conditions where the patient has prepared himself properly. The results would then be valid.

So, too, should a teacher take circumstances into consideration. If for some reason, such as anxiety or illness, the student does poorly, he should be given other opportunities to prove himself in the same task until he can experience success.

This is the basis upon which the so-called "teaching machines" have been built. The machines are programmed to teach a person in the manner which I have been considering. The process begins with a task the student already knows. He answers a question, or performs a task, correctly, and is instructed to go on with the next. As soon as he experiences success with that, he proceeds once again, each step graduated in a way that will help him build up to a successful completion of his goal.

If you want to teach someone something, let him know what it is you expect of him. Give him time to learn it, preferably in his own way and as a result of his own effort and discovery of the principles involved. In that way, it will have meaning for him. To find out if he has mastered it, ask him to perform the same task for you.

The more routine an experience becomes, the easier it is to handle. This helps to avoid stress and worry. A child who knows how to cope with stress should be able to function fairly well in most situations. If a child is encouraged instead of criticized, he will be more willing to try new tasks.

As teachers and parents, it is our responsibility to see that children have the chance to do as many things as they can. We can help by encouraging them, and by offering instruction if they request it. It is wise to let them "try their wings," for if a child believes he can succeeed on his own, he probably will.

——— RECOMMENDED READING

Birney, Robert Charles. *Fear of Failure*. New York: Van Nostrand-Reinhold Co., 1969.

Gallagher, Patricia A. *Positive Classroom Performance Techniques for Changing Behavior*. Denver: Love Publishing Co., 1971.

Gray, Jeffrey A. *The Psychology of Fear and Stress*. New York: McGraw-Hill, 1971.

Mink, Oscar G. *The Behavior Change Process*. (Programmed Instruction). New York: Harper & Row, 1970.

Schneer, Henry Irving. *The Asthmatic Child–Psychosomatic Approach to Problems and Treatment*. New York: Harper & Row, 1963.

chapter 10

Tim

(A PROBLEM OF DEALING WITH A PARENT'S DEATH)

Tim was a joyous boy who always contributed to classroom activities and volunteered for even the most arduous tasks. The children liked him, for he had a sense of fairness and always remembered to take turns when choosing partners or playing games.

Then something happened to change him. His father died. His grandmother telephoned the school to inform us that Tim would be absent for a few days because of his father's sudden death. I wondered how he would react when he came back after the funeral. More important, I wondered how I should react to Tim, whether I should cater to him at first, or try to be as normal as possible.

When he returned, he seemed to be all right at first. Because he did not mention his father's death, I decided to refrain from saying anything about it, but rather to wait until he brought up the subject. He was eager to catch up on his work. While the other children played games at free time, Tim studied the classroom encyclopedias and worked at the science table. There seemed to be no time for him to dwell on his grief, if, indeed, he was feeling that emotion. I had recently lost my own father, and knew what bereavement could mean. However, I knew the feelings of an adult, not a child.

Within a few weeks, Tim's behavior changed from that of a cooperative, sensible eight-year-old boy to a troublesome menace. His work became careless, and his appearance was unruly. He seldom combed his hair or cleaned his shoes. He often tracked mud into the room and became surly when I asked him to clean up the floor. He laughed loudly at anyone who made a simple mistake. He became impatient and aggressive. I noticed that he tore or wrinkled papers he was asked to distribute to the children. When he came to school late, he wore an expression that dared me to question his reason. It was obvious that Tim was seeking attention. That meant he needed help.

Because Tim had been a well-behaved boy up until then, and because the reason for his behavior seemed to be connected with his father's death, I decided that he did not require the services of a psychologist immediately. We would allow some more time to pass, so that he had a chance to make an adjustment. If, later on, he was still severely troubled, we could make an appointment for his emotional evaluation.

I wanted to investigate his home situation first. Numerous telephone calls to his mother proved useless. She was neither able to talk on the telephone nor able to visit the school because she had three younger children at home. From the remarks she made over the phone, it seemed obvious that she did not care about Tim's school behavior. This may have been a result of her own grief, as her tense voice and the rapid flow of words seemed to indicate the tension she was under.

I debated with myself the advisability of paying a visit to Tim's house. Eventually a good opportunity presented itself. Tim missed the school bus one afternoon. He had been loitering in the boys' lavatory at dismissal time and had not heard the bell. Instead of reprimanding him for "fooling around," I offered to drive him home.

When I telephoned his mother to ask her permission to take him home in my car, she seemed relieved that she would not have to pay taxi fare. Perhaps she was glad to be warned of my visit, for I hinted at my desire to talk with her about Tim's behavior in school and the change in his work habits and attitudes.

When Tim and I arrived at his house, he immediately retreated to his room, without even greeting his mother. At first, she seemed uneasy in my presence, making vague comments about the other children who were two, four and six.

When I mentioned Tim's unusual behavior in school, she admitted that he had seemed "strange" since his father's death. She said that she had tried to shield him from the "brutal facts." I asked her what she meant. She explained that all four children had been sent to a relative's home during the mourning period, and that they did not attend the funeral. She felt that seeing their father in a casket at a funeral home might leave a permanent scar upon them. She was especially concerned about Tim who was the eldest and thus may have had some understanding of the finality of death.

When I asked her the cause of her husband's death, she told me a long story. It provided evidence that Tim had suffered much more pain than any funeral rituals could have imposed.

On the way home from a summer evening's drive, the family car had developed a punctured tire. Tim's father pulled into a service station to have it repaired. The attendant was busy pumping gas, so Tim's father proceeded to replace the tire himself. His mother and the children went to a vending machine nearby for soda pop. Tim turned around and, noticing his father on the ground, shouted, "Daddy looks dead!"

His mother scolded him for scaring her. She thought her husband was merely lying on the pavement to replace the tire. A glance at him, however, caused her to utter a scream, for he had fallen to the ground, gripping his chest, and his face was turning blue.

Her utterance brought the attendant to her side. Although an ambulance was summoned immediately, Tim's father died of an acute coronary attack before the vehicle arrived. Because the death occurred on public property, the body had to remain where it was until it could be examined by a coroner. The ambulance attendants covered the body with a white paper shroud while a small crowd of curious onlookers gathered around. A light drizzle began to fall as twilight descended and the long wait commenced.

The service station's manager arrived and decided to close the station for the night, as the presence of the body on the pavement would undoubtedly discourage business. He wanted to turn off the glaring overhead lights and disperse the crowd. When he saw the frightened look on the faces of the children, he reluctantly switched off the lights, but left the office illuminated.

He offered to drive Tim's mother and the children home, but she refused because the coroner had not yet arrived, and she did not want to leave her husband's body. The children had

72

drunk soda pop and needed to use the rest rooms. The kindly manager took the boys into the men's room and washed off their faces and hands with soothing warm water. Then he gave them candy bars from the office vending machine. Because Tim's mother did not know how to drive, he started the car and let the engine run so the heater could warm up the shivering children.

His kind words touched the mother's heart, and she began to sob hysterically. This frightened the children even more. By the time their aunt arrived to take them home with her, they were in a state of bewilderment.

The children remained at their aunt's house for the next few days. Tim's mother felt that they had been through enough misery without adding the shock of a funeral. She considered them too young to be exposed to any aspect of mourning. Besides, she felt that it would be easier for her if the children were taken care of. She had enough to do, and she did not like the idea of having the children see her so upset. After the funeral, the children returned home where their mother tried to make everything the same as they remembered it. However, naturally, it was not the same, because their father was missing.

As I listened to her story, I began to understand what had happened to Tim. First, he had received a shock by seeing his father drop over dead. He had been exposed to a frightening episode of waiting in a car in a strange place at night, and then been whisked away from his mother. He had lost his father, and, in a sense, his mother, too. Just at a time when he needed her presence and reassurance, she sent him away.

I was convinced that Tim was the kind of boy who would have been a help to his mother during the period between his father's death and the funeral. Not all children would be capable of bearing such a burden, but Tim was intelligent and basically stable and, in his childish fashion, he seemed capable of understanding the situation.

He loved his mother and naturally wanted to be with her. When he was sent away, he probably felt rejected, perhaps even punished, if he recalled that she had scolded him for scaring her.

When Tim's mother and I talked this over, she began to understand Tim's feelings. She had been so upset herself that she had failed to consider the children in the proper perspective. At the time, she had done what she thought to be best for them.

We both agreed to encourage Tim to talk about the incident rather than keep it bottled up inside. We discussed ways in which he could help her now, for it was not too late to begin. It was important to think of Tim as a child and not impose adult standards and responsibilities upon him. Many people will inform a boy in Tim's circumstances that he is "the man of the family now," and the sense of responsibility that is produced by that state often creates overwhelming anxieties in a child.

Because Tim's mother was learning to drive a car, she decided to let Tim help her prepare for the driver's test. He was good at reading, so they went over the drivers' manual together. He asked her questions and she gave him answers. (In a way, he was helping her adjust to the new situation as much as she was helping him.) He also washed the car, and cleaned out the garage, useful activities that provided a safe outlet for his pent-up emotions. When his mother obtained her driver's license, he was proud that he had been so helpful.

She, in turn, reassured him about how much she needed his help and understanding. She had been afraid to learn to operate a car. He had told her there was nothing to it. Because of his confidence in her, she was successful. They both profited by their aid to one another.

Tim eventually began to feel that he was an important, integral part of the family unit, a feeling he had lost when he was left out of the mourning situation. His mother realized that it might have been desirable for him to have been with her at the funeral and to have shared in all the feelings that accompanied his father's death. Then his grief would have been openly expressed instead of repressed.

With the younger children, of course, the situation was different. They were not capable of behaving the way Tim did. Yet, Tim could have helped them, too, by openly participating in the funeral arrangements, and then explaining to them, in his own way, what was involved. Children often can see the world better through the eyes of another child.

Several months went by during which Tim showed daily improvement in school. He still did not talk about his father to me or to the children, but he was once again his old, outgoing self. He *did* mention that his mother had obtained her driver's license and that they bought their gasoline at the service station operated by their good "friend." When I asked his mother about this, she informed me that the "friend" was the kindly gas station manager who had aided them on the night of her husband's death.

At the approach of Father's Day, the children prepared to make gifts for the occasion. There were other children than Tim who had no fathers and they decided to present their gifts to men they knew such as a favorite uncle, grandfather or neighbor. I decided it was time to test Tim. While he worked on his gift, I asked him who was going to receive it. He said he was making it for his friend at the gas station as a thank-you gift.

"Thank-you for what?" I asked.

"For being so good to us when my father died," he explained.

This was the first time Tim had mentioned his father's death to me, and he did it freely, without morbidity. Of course, he missed his father, yet I could see that he was going forward and looking to the future in a way that appeared to indicate normal healing.

COMMENTS

It is usually difficult for young children to deal with death. This is partly because they do not fully understand its implications, and also because they do not have the emotional maturity to approach it realistically. Each child will react differently to the event, according to his home situation, personality and disposition, and to the reaction of his family.

In dealing with a child in such circumstances, a conservative program is generally desirable. Extreme overt sympathy and relaxation of all forms of discipline tend to pamper the child. On the other hand, overly strict discipline and an insistence upon immediate return to previously performed activities could easily drive a child toward the development of undesirable behavior.

It is usually best to wait a reasonable time, allowing the child to return to his normal emotional climate at his own pace. All the while, encouragement should be offered when it is needed. An important aspect of helping a child to overcome his grief is to provide him with meaningful activities as soon as he can tolerate them. Time is your best ally. Patience on the part of teacher and parent can do much to generate the desire for readjustment on the part of the child. Force at any point usually tends to discourage a child, especially if he is sensitive.

It is good to show the child in some way that he is not alone in his feelings and fears. If the child knows that others have experienced similar emotions, it may help him feel that he is not as different as he fears he may be.

While some persons feel that children should be spared the "facts of death," it is becoming more usual to allow children to learn from the experience by participating in the family's grieving. If sent away to distant relatives or friends, for example, the child may feel abandoned at a time when he needs more than ever to be close to his immediate family. By participating in the funeral, he can find an outlet for his emotions and acquire a feeling that he is an important member of his family.

If you are not sure what to do in a particular case, it may be advisable to check with a clergyman or funeral director. They can offer advice based upon the experiences of many people who have been involved in funerals.

Some adults do not like to think about death. They postpone making wills, or they have no idea what their insurance policies cover. Despite the fact that death is inevitable, they would rather think about more pleasant subjects.

Children, on the other hand, are often curious about death and wish to talk about it. They may see a dog run over by a car, or a bird that has fallen from a tree, and wonder why it has stopped living. Often they ask numerous questions. If we can answer those questions intelligently, their curiosity will be satisfied. And, if we can prepare them to accept death as an inevitable part of living, we will help them to develop a healthy philosophy that will enable them to meet future problems with some confidence.

Most important, our own reactions and attitudes to events play a great part in developing the child's feelings. Too much or too little compassion and sympathy may be detrimental to a child who is going through a crisis such as death.

A good way to help a child is to know him. For example, the way he reacts in other situations often reveals how he will react under emergency or crisis conditions. If you also let him know you, he will gain confidence in you and sense that you are sincere and are acting in his best interests.

——— RECOMMENDED READING

Furman, Erna. *A Child's Parent Dies*. New Haven: Yale University Press, 1974.

Grollman, Earl A. *Explaining Death to Children*. Boston: Beacon Press, 1967.

———. *Talking About Death* (A Dialogue between Parent and Child). Boston: Beacon Press, 1970.

Ogg, Elizabeth. *A Death in the Family*. New York: Public Affairs Committee, 1976.

Stein, Sara Bonnett et al. *About Dying*. New York: Walker and Company, 1974.

chapter 11

Darlene
(A PROBLEM OF FACING DEATH)

Before I knew the truth about Darlene, I thought that her mother was keeping her out of school for the most trivial reasons. The written excuses Darlene usually gave me read: *Please excuse Darlene. She seemed tired so I let her sleep in.*

Many children in my classroom at that time watched late television shows. They knew how to persuade a weary mother to let them skip school the following day. Darlene, however, seldom mentioned television programs that were broadcast later than the usual bedtime. The flimsy excuses Darlene gave me thus aroused my curiosity.

I could not understand why a child would be tired so frequently. Darlene looked healthy, except for a pale, somewhat translucent complexion which I did not consider too uncommon in a blond child. Because she was missing so much school, I asked the attendance officer to investigate.

The report he brought back shocked me. Darlene was a victim of leukemia, not the kind that kills in a few weeks, but rather a chronic form that was being kept under control by treatments.

Darlene's mother thought it best not to tell anyone, especially Darlene's brothers and sisters, for fear that the information might be inadvertently passed on to Darlene. In her mother's opinion, it was essential for Darlene to continue living as normally and happily as possible. The family doctor and the specialists who were treating Darlene agreed that it was desirable to keep Darlene in school whenever she was able to attend.

Her life followed a fairly regular pattern. She attended school every day for a few weeks. Then she was absent for a day or two, followed by a longer absence lasting more than a week.

Ultimately she returned, vigorous and willing to work, until the cycle repeated itself.

During her absences, Darlene went to the out-patient department of a local children's hospital where she was given chemotherapy and blood transfusions. After several days of bed rest, she was able to resume her activities.

Although Darlene felt no pain, she was overcome by extreme weakness and lassitude when the disease was rampant within her. Before I knew the cause, I had interpreted her behavior as an indication of laziness or boredom.

After one particularly severe bout, she began to lose her hair. Day after day she appeared with less and less hair, until she was practically bald. The children in the classroom were curious to know what was causing it. As there had been an epidemic of head lice in the school, many of them thought that Darlene's mother may have tried some kind of strong treatment for "bug removal."

Darlene, however, was unwilling to allow anyone to think she had "bugs" in her hair. She simply told the truth, at least as much of it as she knew, explaining that she had X-rays and had "got burned." Most of the children had received X-rays at their dentists at one time or another and, knowing how strong radiation was, accepted her explanation.

A few unkind children called her "egghead" and other names which she did not seem to mind. I wondered if she was too tired and weak to care what they said. I began to pity her until I realized that I could not help her in that way; it was important for me to do as her mother wished.

All the while, however, I had the distinct feeling that Darlene sensed her predicament. Because she was just nine years old, the technical term *poor prognosis* probably meant nothing to her. Yet, she may have been alerted by the doctor's tone of voice or facial expression when he had discussed the case with her mother.

What made me feel this way was Darlene's habit of going to the classroom mirror and staring at her reflection for long intervals. Sometimes she touched the mirror, then her face, as if to reassure herself that she was still there. It may have been my imagination, but as her disease became worse, her trips to the mirror increased. The children probably thought she was concerned about the returning growth of her hair which, after four months, had begun to grow in again, fine and blond. Although that may have been the reason, I doubted it, for she seldom looked at her hair. It was always her hands and face that she studied and touched.

It was difficult for me to react to her in the same way in which I treated the others, but I did not want to single her out as exceptional. Whenever she behaved in a naughty manner, she was obliged to pay for it by being denied a privilege. At those times, she would sulk, which caused me to wonder if her mother was more lenient than she admitted with Darlene at home.

One day I realized that Darlene probably suspected the serious nature of her illness. The children were describing their future ambitions. When it was Darlene's turn, she commented, "I'd like to be a teacher, if I live that long." It was not a flippant remark; on the contrary, she said it with genuine sadness. Fortunately, a boy veered the mood into another direction by proclaiming, "Teachers' jobs make them *seem* old. They don't really live *that* long!"

During Darlene's absences, I kept a file containing the assignments she had missed so that she could catch up when she returned. I was reluctant to give her too much work for fear of overtaxing her strength. Because she was a bright child and realized what she had missed, I had to be careful. Occasionally she caught me "forgetting" some difficult material which she had observed the others doing. Rather than make her more conspicuous than she already was, I began to give her all the work expected of the children in her class. She did the work faithfully when she was able to do so. I feel that she appreciated the demands which I imposed upon her.

One afternoon, she remained after school to help wash the chalkboards. Pausing before my desk and glancing at her reflection in the pail of water she held, she said, "May I ask you something important?"

When I nodded, she continued, "Are you afraid to die?"

The suddenness of her question caught me unprepared. I am certain she realized how flustered I felt at that moment.

It was obvious that Darlene needed someone to share her

fears, and it was also apparent, after we had talked for a while, that she was quite aware of her predicament. I learned that she was keeping her anxiety to herself because she did not want to worry her family.

"They are so happy all the time," she said. "I hate to spoil their fun." That "fun," of course, was their way of hiding the truth from her.

At the time it was difficult for me to realize that a young child could possess such insight. After talking with Darlene, I knew I must speak to her mother, for we obviously had been approaching Darlene's problem unwisely.

Conferences were set up with Darlene's parents, doctors and a psychiatrist. The psychiatrist explained that Darlene was the kind of individual who preferred to know the facts. While we were reasonably certain that she did not understand the full implications of fatality, we were sure that she appreciated sharing her fears openly with others. We agreed to tell Darlene all we could, at least all that we felt she was able to handle emotionally.

She was told that she had leukemia and that there was no cure for the disease at the present time. However, her hopes for eventual recovery were kept alive by assuring her that research was going on continuously and that the disease would some day be under control.

We discussed serious diseases in the classroom and read books about diseases that had formerly been considered incurable, such as smallpox, diphtheria and polio. The children had been vaccinated against smallpox, and had received other immunization shots. They knew something about resistance to disease, and wished to learn more.

They began to read books about medical research workers such as Pasteur, Lister and Wasserman. We showed films and filmstrips which detailed the lives of science's heroes. We obtained health books at the school library and at various public libraries, and incorporated Darlene's personal problem into our curriculum.

Whenever telethons were broadcast to collect funds for diseases such as leukemia, muscular dystrophy or birth defects, the children watched with interest, for they began to realize that everyone can help medical research in one way or another. The most important immediate fact was that research was going on, research that would possibly help Darlene.

Darlene began to believe and hope, and so did we. Her parents began to treat Darlene as a "normal" child, and Darlene, in turn, responded in a positive way. Some medical experts believe that emotions often control a body's chemistry, which in turn influences disease patterns. Cases have been reported in which patients suffering from incurable cancers suddenly began to recover "for no apparent reason." In earlier eras, such occurrences had been considered "miracles."

Darlene's youth and optimism, along with the understanding and compassion of those about her, helped her to adjust to her situation. As of this writing, she is still alive—no better, but then again, no worse, and she is hoping for an eventual breakthrough to a complete cure.

COMMENTS

You will notice that we did not actually come right out and say to Darlene, "You have about two years to live." Such a comment would be difficult even for a mature adult to accept. Most of us want to live and we hang on to hope, no matter how slender the thread. Even an unconscious patient on an operating table fights for his life as every cell of his body seems programmed to live.

It is difficult to determine how any given individual will react to the fact of his own impending death. Some people need to know the truth so that they can "set their house in order." Others are content to live in a state of oblivion; in fact, many people refuse to consult a doctor if they suspect cancer. They would rather maintain false hope than have their hope shattered by real facts.

If a child is involved, the problem is more complex, and we must take into consideration the maturity of the child as well as his personality. In Darlene's case, I felt that her mother had underestimated Darlene's ability to comprehend the situation. Darlene's statement about wanting to be a teacher "if she lived that long" indicated to me that she had some insight into her situation.

Certain children, such as Darlene, are capable of handling such a situation *if* the facts are presented in a manner that they can understand and accept. Many psychologists with whom I have conferred agree that holding in fears and anxieties can be worse for the child's sense of well-being than an awareness of the facts.

In some instances, the illness can often become worse because the child worries so much. As an example, a boy with a congenital heart disease was not told that he would have to go through open-heart surgery. During his frequent visits to a doctor, his overprotective parents fooled him into a false sense of well-being by minimizing his condition.

At first he was happy in his state of oblivion. However, he began to worry when his parents would not allow him to swim, dive or play football with his friends. As his condition became worse, he began to feel frightened by his breathlessness. He was also concerned over his fingernails, which appeared blue at times. When he asked his mother about it, she lied and told him he "took after her,"adding that her funny fingernails were disguised by bright red nail enamel.

Secretly, the boy worried himself sick—or sicker than he might have been had he been told what to expect. He went to the hospital totally unprepared for the experience. Although the surgery was fortunately a success, his recovery time might have been shorter had he been in a more positive frame of mind.

In contrast, another boy was told the facts by his parents and doctors. He was informed that his heart had a tiny hole which leaked and needed mending. The surgeon showed him a plastic model of the human heart and pointed out exactly what would be done to remedy his condition, explaining how the "hole" in his heart would be mended. The boy had a rubber raft which had sprung a leak and been patched. Thus he could relate the surgical experience to something familiar. The fact that his rubber raft was completely safe to use after its repair job gave him confidence in a procedure that was obviously similar.

Of course, the doctor's entire explanation was expressed in oversimplified, elementary terms. As a result, the child understood that, like the rubber raft with a leak, he could not work for any great length of time or be treated roughly. Thus, he played quietly and chose inactive games while waiting for his day in surgery.

The positive aspects of the operation were emphasized. No one mentioned that his heart would be stopped while his body was connected to the heart-lung machine which pumped donor blood to sustain him during the procedure. That might have frightened him, for he was old enough to know that a stopped heart generally means death.

It is interesting to note at this point how many clergymen with whom I have talked in reference to a child's self-awareness of death, shy away from a certain prayer which many well-meaning parents teach their children.

The prayer is:

> Now I lay me down to sleep,
> I pray the Lord my soul to keep.
> If I should die before I wake,
> I pray the Lord my soul to take.

It is, of course, meant to be reassuring. Nevertheless, young children who repeat it night after night just before falling asleep may come to associate sleep with death. Some psychologists have mentioned that insomnia or nightmares in certain children may be a direct result of this, or a similar, bedtime thought.

Thus it is to the child's advantage to be taught the philosophy behind the words. Simply learning the words by rote can be detrimental in some instances.

The essential thing is to have the child understand. How can we prepare a young child to understand so serious a matter as death? As a result of my association with Darlene, I have put together some ideas which are designed to help teachers and parents who may be confronted by the task of preparing such a child:

1. Prepare yourself first. Learn as much as you can of the facts of the matter. Then put them as simply as possible to the child so he or she can understand them. You need to speak with doctors, psychologists or clergymen before approaching the child. It is essential to know in

advance what you will tell the child, and how much you will not tell him.

2. Know how much the child can take and accept. That will depend on his age, intelligence, experience and emotional maturity. It will also depend on the relationship you have developed with the child. Thus, the better you get to know the child *during normal conditions*, the easier it will be for you to relate to him in critical situations.

3. Be consistent. Encourage all others connected with the child to behave in the same manner in which you are acting. If you do not do this, the child will become confused and more frightened than he needs to be.

4. Try to avoid extremes. Some adults cater to every whim of a disabled child, while others try to be overly strict for fear the child will suspect something is wrong. Strike a happy medium if possible.

5. Remember that each child is a unique individual with special needs. You, as an understanding adult, can help the child meet those needs by helping him live day by day, pleasantly and profitably, making the most of the present.

In some cases, the present is all the child has. It is a difficult task to be objective when faced with such a problem. Therefore, you will need all the help that you can get. Seek it from whatever source best matches your own philosophy, but be open-minded enough to change your views if it seems in the child's best interest.

RECOMMENDED READING

Anthony, Elwyn James and Cyrille Koupernik. *The Impact of Disease and Death*. New York: Wiley, 1973.

Anthony, Helen Sylvia. *The Discovery of Death in Childhood*. New York: Basic Books, 1972.

Cook, Sarah S. *Children and Dying*. New York: Health Sciences Publication Corp., 1974.

Creer, Thomas L. and Walter P. Christian. *Chronically Ill and Handicapped Children, Their Management and Rehabilitation.* Champaign, Ill.: Research Press Co., 1976.

Kubler-Ross, Elisabeth. *On Death and Dying.* New York: MacMillan Publishing Company, 1969.

Neal, Robert E. *The Art of Dying.* New York: Harper & Row, 1973.

Reed, Elizabeth Liggett. *Helping Children With the Mystery of Death.* Nashville: Abdingdon Press, 1970.

Zeligs, Rose. *Children's Experience With Death.* Springfield, Ill.: C.C. Thomas, 1974.

chapter 12

Amy
(A PROBLEM OF PHYSICAL PRECOCITY)

One of the girls in my third grade classroom was intensely shy about removing her outer clothing to prepare for gym. At that time, the primary grade boys and girls were given physical education classes together and were taught by the boys' gym teacher. Usually, none of the children seemed to mind the coeducational feature of the activities. Many enjoyed the balanced mixture of active games and relatively quiet activities, ranging from basketball to folk dancing.

Some children that age are modest, so we usually managed to simulate an atmosphere of privacy in the classroom by turning out the lights as the children took off their top shirts, skirts and sweaters. At those times, Amy asked to go to the lavatory to change her clothes. Occasionally she pleaded a sore foot or a headache, conditions which excused her from taking gym altogether. At certain times she asked if she could remain in the room to read a book instead of going to gym. As she did not ordinarily like to read, I concluded that she objected to some aspect of the physical education program and wished to avoid it. But why was she receptive to it sometimes, and not at others? When I asked the gym teacher about her behavior in his class, he informed me that she participated wholeheartedly when she went. The problem was that she was not consistent in her feelings about it.

Other instances puzzled me about Amy. There were times when she asked to be excused from the room to use the lavatory several times a day. These "emergencies" came and went with disturbing regularity, though some weeks Amy would be content to go to recess with the other girls, usually once in the morning and again in the afternoon. I began to wonder if Amy had home troubles that made her nervous. There had been a child in my classroom a few years before who became upset at the end of each month because his father paid the family a visit. His parents were separated, and the boy obviously disliked the visits for some reason, and became tense enough to suffer from mild diarrhea. It was not impossible that Amy had some similar problem at home.

I decided to watch Amy's habits more closely. Although she was friendly with girls rather than boys, she avoided even the girls occasionally. Once in a while she accompanied the girls to recess, only to ask to be excused upon returning to the classroom. Usually she asked to get another drink of water, claiming to be thirsty. Something pleading in her manner always caused me to allow her to return to the lavatory.

I began to suspect that she might be up to some kind of mischief in the lavatory. Sometimes a child watches for a friend to pass a classroom and gives a signal to meet him in the corridor. If a teacher is not alert, a child may be permitted to leave the room, join his friend and get into some illegal or forbidden activity, such as buying or selling stolen items, smoking cigarettes or marijuana, popping pills or simply writing naughty words on the walls with felt pens.

I did not believe that Amy was capable of any real wrongdoing because she seemed too embarrassed when she asked to leave the room. I considered the fact that she might be overly shy because she was the only Puerto Rican girl in my third grade. If she felt different from the other children, it would explain a great deal.

Because she was a minority of one, the other girls might have been curious to see whether or not she was anatomically "like them." Most of the girls "traded looks" at one time or another. They used the booths in the lavatory to examine one another and then, satisfied that they were no different from each other, they ceased to be interested. They were at an exploratory age with a normal, healthy curiosity about the human body. Amy may have sensed their curiosity, misinterpreted it and wished to avoid their scrutiny.

Upon one occasion Amy stayed longer than usual in the lavatory. I began to worry that she might have become ill. When the room helper was sent out to investigate, she returned and informed me that Amy was in a booth, crying, and that she refused to come out. I summoned an aide to watch my class for a few minutes and went to the girls' lavatory to find out what was the matter.

All was quiet when I entered. The doors to all the booths were closed. They are lock-protected; a teacher with a special key can open them from the outside, even if they are locked from the inside. I unlocked them, one by one, and found them all empty except the one near the far wall. Amy was there, leaning forlornly against the tile wall, her face pale and tear-streaked. When she saw me, she began to sob quietly. I noticed blood running down her leg onto the edge of her white sock. A horrible thought crossed my mind. I had read recently of a case in another school where a pervert had lurked in the girls' lavatory and raped a little girl. "Are you all right?" I asked quickly.

She did not answer.

"What happened?" I asked.

Then I realized that Amy seemed more embarrassed than frightened. She murmured, "Go away. Leave me alone."

I had taught young children for several years but had never before encountered an eight-year-old who had started menstruating. Amy had no outward manifestations of premature development, such as enlarged breasts or the typically adolescent complexion. Consequently, the thought had never entered my mind that she was having her monthly periods all those times when she asked to be excused.

"Is this the first time this has happened?" I asked her. Because it seemed difficult for her to handle, I wanted her to think I had not noticed anything about her in the past.

She shook her head and began to cry again.

"Well, let me help you get cleaned up," I said as matter-of-factly as I could. To help her feel better about the situation, I added, "I always get so mad when it happens to me unexpectedly, don't you?"

Her averted eyes now sought mine. She looked surprised and said, "You mean—*you* do it, too? You do it, and you're not —married?"

I wanted to laugh, but her expression stopped me. The child

was obviously quite ignorant about the facts of life, and scared to death about what was happening to her. I knew I must tell her a great deal. Right then, however, it was important to get her out of the lavatory before any other girls came in.

I took her down the hall to the teachers' lounge, where there is a vending machine for sanitary napkins. There is no such dispenser in the little girls' room, because, theoretically, they do not need such items.

In the lounge I helped Amy get cleaned up and comfortable. The busy activity and my matter-of-fact attitude put her somewhat at ease. Her humiliation momentarily forgotten, she thanked me shyly. On the way back to the classroom, she asked me to promise not to tell anyone about her. I promised, and then added, "How would you like to have lunch with me today, Amy?"

Her expressive brown eyes became bigger than usual. She seemed at a loss for words.

"Why not?" I asked. "You feel all right, don't you? No cramps or anything?"

"You know about the cramps, too?" she asked, astonished.

"Sure. I get them sometimes. All women do. You're really a young woman now, Amy."

She was eager to talk about this. I sensed that she had dozens of questions to ask me. When we returned to the classroom, she seemed reluctant to break off our talk, but she had consented to join me for lunch.

The other children were curious, undoubtedly believing that Amy had been caught in some mischief in the lavatory. Soon, however, our activities took up their attention and, when the lunch bell rang, we all went to the cafeteria.

The children's cafeteria was far too noisy for conversation. Likewise, the teachers' cafeteria was not an ideal place to have a personal talk, so Amy and I returned to the empty classroom with our trays. I hung a sign on the door to insure privacy. As we ate, Amy confided that she had been getting "it" since she turned eight. It was obvious that she did not know what "it" meant. She told me that she was afraid to ask anyone at home.

I discovered that Amy was the eldest girl in a family of five brothers and two sisters. Her mother worked and had little time for her children. Amy had been a baby sitter as long as

90

she could remember, but did not seem to resent the fact. She adored her mother, but was also afraid of her. She noticed that "it" happened to her mother, too, but she assumed that it was caused by being married and that it had something to do with the opposite sex.

Amy rarely had the opportunity to use sanitary napkins; she was afraid to ask her mother for any. Upon occasion, she removed a used one from the garbage can and used it herself. Usually she resorted to using cleaning rags in lieu of napkins.

When I asked her why she was afraid to ask her mother, she said, "She'd holler!"

"Why should she holler?" I asked, in genuine surprise that any woman would not understand the needs of a female.

"Because I'm having—you know," she said shyly.

At that point I sensed an attitude of guilt in Amy's manner. With careful questioning, I learned that she had once let a boy look at and touch her genitalia for 50 cents. She quickly added, "But he didn't do what Mom and Dad do when they are fooling around, honest!"

She went on to explain that she knew the "fooling around" was what caused her mother to bleed at times and get "the bad bellyache." Then she added, "If my mother knew I got it, too, she'd kill me. My aunt fooled around and they threw her out of the house."

"Amy," I told her, "You don't have what you are having today for any other reason than that you are a woman. All women get monthly periods. It's part of growing up. Most girls start when they're about twelve. You have just begun earlier, that's all."

I went on to tell her about myself, how I had not menstruated until I was 14 and how worried I had become when I thought I would never grow up.

We talked about her cousin José whose voice was beginning to change. She felt better to realize that boys have ways in which they turn into men. It helped reassure her that she was just normal. She was eager to learn more, so I told her that we would have further chats from time to time, whenever she wanted to talk.

It was obvious that Amy knew nothing of the menstrual cycle, so in subsequent talks, we discussed its nature and how it prepares women to become mothers. She had no idea of the regularity of the occurrence. I gave her a pretty little pocket calendar on which to keep a record of her periods so that she could estimate future periods and not worry about unexpected accidents. I also assured her that she could borrow sanitary napkins from me until she decided to tell her mother.

I made a mental note to have a talk with the gym teacher and the school nurse. Eventually I wanted to talk with Amy's mother, but I wanted to give Amy a chance to broach the subject to her mother first.

When I told the gym teacher why Amy did not want to participate in gym on certain occasions, he understood and agreed to give Amy tacitly the understanding she needed, without embarrassing her. He mentioned that I might suggest to Amy the importance of mild physical activity on certain days of the month. Eventually, with guidance and understanding, Amy participated willingly in gym, secure in the knowledge that she was not doing anything to hurt herself, and secure that she would not have an embarrassing accident.

Although I told the school nurse, she suggested that we send Amy to the clinic for a talk with her only as a last resort, explaining that a trip to the nurse for menstrual reasons sometimes causes girls to associate a normal function with being ill or indisposed; as a result their "infirmity" eventually causes them to feel worse than the condition warrants.

The nurse gave me a pamphlet for Amy to read, and I decided to keep it until I had a chance to talk to Amy's mother. Amy was still shy about broaching the subject to her mother until I showed her the attractive pamphlet. We went over it often until Amy could read every word and talk about all the illustrations with objectivity. At last she took it home to show to her mother, as an introduction to her situation.

Within a few days, Amy's mother came to school for the talk. She was grateful to learn about Amy and how well she was handling herself. She had no idea of the truth, and, in fact, had considered Amy lazy when she wanted to stay in bed on certain days. Amy and her mother went over the pamphlet many times, and I feel sure that they profited from the experience of sharing its contents.

With her confidence restored, Amy became much more secure in school and at home. Her attendance at school improved, her work rose above normal level, and she became friendly with the children. Toward the end of the school year, she confided in one of her girlfriends. The friend was envious to the point of wearing a sanitary napkin whenever Amy required one, just to feel as grown-up as Amy. This did much to raise Amy's self-esteem and pride, and helped her to realize that precocity need not be a burden.

COMMENTS

Physical maturation sometimes occurs in girls at an early age. Most sex education courses are directed toward girls of 12 or older, since this is the average age for such maturation to occur. However, a wise teacher or parent will become aware of symptoms that may indicate the presence of such maturity.

Headaches, stomach pains, cramps, frequent visits to the lavatory or perhaps an unwillingness to participate in physical activities often suggest such a condition.

Of course, many mothers are aware of their daughters' conditions. Their little girls will be, we hope, better prepared for menstruation than Amy was. However, just because a mother knows what is happening to her daughter she is not necessarily willing, or able, to discuss the problem openly. Despite today's more liberal attitudes toward sex, many women still feel awkward when called upon to discuss intimate feminine facts with their daughters. Some are willing, but unable, to handle the subject with the objectivity or thoroughness it deserves. The responsibility is often placed upon a teacher or nurse and even many teachers may feel reluctant to delve into the subject. Whether or not sex education and allied topics should be taught in school is still controversial and open to discussion. Thus, a teacher who goes into it in too much detail may find herself under attack by a school board or a parent-teacher organization. A safe approach is to communicate with the child's mother and discuss the matter with her before doing anything else.

The school nurse, as I mentioned before, is a good source of information. However, keep in mind that many nurses are busy with sick children, preventive immunization programs, dental hygiene projects and so on. Their work load does not always enable them to do counseling. This may also be true of the family physician. Many doctors now require a "consultation appointment" for such matters.

A child who matures young is bound to feel different from others in the same age group. Restrictions are placed upon her at certain times which are not placed upon her peers.

An important aspect of dealing with a situation of this sort is to put emphasis on the normality of the occurrence. It helps if the child who has fears and doubts has someone with whom to identify. A woman teacher whom the child admires and trusts, for example, can share her own experiences with the child. If the child knows that someone else has gone through the same kind of experience, she is consoled.

Men teachers who notice symptoms in a little girl student can refer the child to the school nurse or to a woman teacher in whom the child has confidence. A former teacher for whom the child has shown real fondness would be a good choice. The male teacher can readily determine who taught the youngster in previous years, get into a discussion about favorite teachers with the child, and then refer the child to the teacher of her choice.

Many pharmaceutical companies prepare booklets to explain menstruation. While they are written for a higher reading level than that of a very young child, teachers and mothers can go over the material with the child. If the child has older sisters, they may look over the booklet and help explain its contents. In many instances, the booklets may also clarify some problems for older girls. With the emphasis in today's schools on corrective reading, many brochures are written in simplified style to accommodate a reading public that is not well versed in sophisticated phraseology. Thus, much of the content can be read by a younger child when she is ready for the material.

If a class in Sexual Maturation is being conducted in your school, ask to let the young child sit in. If her body is ready, her emotions should also be ready and willing to accept pertinent information that will help alleviate her fears by answering her questions. Often the older girls in the group will prove helpful, especially those who have matured early themselves.

We should try to avoid showing embarrassment. We are dealing with a normal, human experience. If the matter is treated with the right mixture of objectivity and warmth, and is kept in good taste, this difficult interval for the extremely young girl can be a profitable one.

Secrecy, embarrassment or ridicule may often result in feelings of guilt. This can color a child's attitudes toward her sexual identity and could possibly lead to serious sexual problems later in life. Fortunately, most girls mature at an older age than Amy did. Amy's precocity could have made her an unhappy person if we had not intervened in time. It is important that we keep in mind the necessity of helping girls of *any* age who are going through this period; some may be physically mature at, say, age 14, but remain emotionally immature. Consequently, the ways in which we have dealt with Amy may be helpful to any child at any stage of her development.

RECOMMENDED READING

Hettlinger, Richard P. *Growing Up With Sex*. New York: Seabury Press, 1971.

Leokum, Arkady, *Tell Me Why*. New York: Grosset & Dunlap, Inc., 1974.

Lerrigo, Marion Olive. *A Story About You*. New York: E.P. Dutton & Co., Inc., 1969.

Pomeroy, Wardell Baxter. *Girls and Sex*. New York: Delacorte Press, 1970.

Seruga, Flora C. et al. *Sex and Sex Education: A Bibliography*. New York: R.R. Bowker Co., 1972.

Sheffield, Margaret. *Where Do Babies Come From?* New York: Alfred A. Knopf, Inc., 1973.

chapter 13

John
(A PROBLEM OF REJECTION)

John was a troublemaker in school. He usually started fights by saying offensive things to other boys, or by holding up his fingers in "dirty" signals. They retaliated by hitting him. It was almost as if he dared them to hurt him, and, when he was beaten by them, he went crying to his grandmother. She became so upset about the boys "picking on" her grandson that she accompanied him to school amost every day.

His record card showed that his parents were divorced and that he was living in the custody of his paternal grandparents. He had failed third grade and was repeating a year in my classroom. No subject interested him. Whenever a topic was introduced, he made faces and put his fingers in his ears. Sometimes he said, "Not that again!" and made ugly sounds, as if he were suffering acutely from some kind of pain.

During study work periods John wandered about the room instead of remaining at his desk to do the assignments. Occasionally he ran out into the corridor and made whooping sounds to attract passers-by. At times he talked noisily and bothered the children who were trying to work. At other times, especially when the children were discussing family activities, John sat at his desk and pouted, his mood sullen and introspective.

The former third grade teacher had not allowed him to go on field trips because of his disruptive behavior. She told me that he had run up and down the aisle on the bus, and had poked his hands out the bus windows. Upon one occasion he had tapped the bus driver on the shoulder while the bus was in motion until, at last, the driver stopped the vehicle and ordered John to sit down or get off the bus. After that, the teacher had told him he would not be invited on any more trips. He pleaded one more chance and she relented. However, the next time was even worse, so she decided to have him remain in school whenever his classmates went on a trip.

I was acquainted with John before he came to my classroom, because the previous year I had offered to let him visit my classroom when he was excluded from field trips. During these visits, he behaved well, something his regular teacher had predicted, claiming that the novelty would keep his interest for a brief time. I could not believe that the nicely behaved little boy who visited my room from time to time was actually the "pest" who "bugged the bus driver," and I suspected that his teacher was being unfair to him. At those moments when I secretly criticized her, I did not know what she was faced with, day after day. When John was permanently assigned to my room the following year, I was at a loss for what to do to control him. I began to admire his previous teacher for having taught him all the skills he had learned. I certainly was not getting any place with him.

In keeping with John's former teacher's policy of excluding him from field trips, I was about to send a note home to his grandmother telling her John could not go with us to the local United States Coast Guard Station, when his grandmother appeared at the classroom door. She was an elderly woman, frail appearing, and soft spoken. I explained that the visit would include an inspection of radar equipment and other technical devices, and that the officers in charge had emphasized the importance of merely looking at, not touching the installations.

I told her that I felt badly about excluding John, as he had been left out of so many activities, but I was afraid that he would do something harmful, either to himself or to the equipment. If his behavior continued in that manner, he certainly had little chance of ever proving himself.

His grandmother suggested a possible solution. She volunteered to accompany the class as one of the chaperones. Her services had been offered in the past, but because she was older than most mothers, the teachers had not accepted her. Her appearance suggested that she might be unable to control even a small group of active children. However, we needed three adults and as I had only two mothers who were able to go with us, she became the third chaperone.

The bus ride to the waterfront station took about 30 minutes.

To my consternation, John's grandmother did not sit with him, but placed herself beside me. She did not seem to pay any attention to the children, as the other chaperones were doing. Nevertheless, I noticed that John was well behaved in the presence of his grandmother. He shared a seat with a boy who usually fought with him, and they talked and pointed out various places of interest along the way.

Ultimately, the seating arrangement turned out to be a fortunate circumstance. John's grandmother told me a great deal about his family background, going into details that were not on his record cards.

John's mother left, admitting that she had no interest in her husband, her home or her child. John's father asked his parents to look after the baby until he could make arrangements for a reconciliation. John stayed at his grandparents' house during the day while his father was at work. Then he began to spend weekends there while the father went bowling or golfing. Soon John was living with his grandparents all the time, and his parents were divorced.

John's father met a young woman who moved in with him. It became evident that he wished to assume no responsibility for the child. Despite the fact that John's grandparents disapproved of the situation, they consented to raise their grandson without his father's help, for they wished to keep peace and spare the boy they loved from any further pain.

John's grandparents, by then in their late 60's, tried their best to keep up with the active, energetic nine-year old boy. (I was not even half that age and found him tiring beyond belief, which made me wonder how the elderly couple managed to put up with him around the clock.)

The only activity John liked was camping. Somehow, his grandparents mustered up enough energy for a week's camping trip in Canada each summer. John lived for that week. He talked about the previous summers; he anticipated the approaching summer; he did not seem to object to being with two old people, as long as he could camp in the big outdoors, cook his food over a fireplace, and sleep in a tent. I had to commend his grandparents, for not many people of any age would risk a week in the woods with a lively boy as their sole companion.

John's grandmother told me more and more about his life and

as I listened, and as the bus rolled on toward our destination, I began to understand some of the reasons why, when another boy proudly announced an activity he had shared with his father, John invariably became disruptive, silly or noisy.

Although he loved his grandparents dearly and was quite dependent upon them emotionally, he was still a child without real parents. Other children in his class had parents, or at least one real parent. Many had grandparents as well; some even had two sets of grandparents.

In addition, many had brothers and sisters, and even those who were "only" children seemed to have friends. On the street where John lived there were no children his age. He had to choose between playing outdoors alone or indoors with only his grandparents for company.

After reviewing many aspects of John's case, I suggested that his grandmother allow John to join a club for boys, such as the Cub Scouts, with a male leader. Such a man could act as the needed father image which the boy so desperately craved. We made arrangements for John to attend a meeting. Since John's grandfather disliked driving at night, a boy's father offered to call for John and drive him to and from the first meeting. John immediately showed enthusiasm for the club. When he learned that the boys planned to go camping, he was ecstatic.

John asked me if I thought his grandparents would be hurt if he went camping with the "guys" instead of with them. I knew how relieved his grandparents would be but I did not want to let John think he was being manipulated, so I assured him that they would understand, provided that he behaved himself at camp. For weeks, all John talked about was summer camp with the boys. His classmates soon shared his enthusiasm. As a result of increased enthusiasm in one subject, John's overall interest in schoolwork increased, and that work improved visibly. Instead of his usual apathy, caused possibly by the fact that he was repeating a grade and considered much of the work repetitious, he began to share ideas with the children.

He still did not have any after-school friends, though. At a parent-teacher meeting, I talked with a few parents about John's loneliness. They offered a suggestion. One family invited John to spend Friday night and all day Saturday at their home. In return, John could invite their son to stay with him for a similar interval.

John's grandparents were delighted and the project worked to their advantage as well as John's. John was invited to spend other weekends at various homes. John's grandmother had to entertain a guest of John's only once in every six weeks, giving the couple several weekends to themselves, during which time they could recover from the hectic pace of living with a young, active boy. Meanwhile, John had the much-needed companionship that was to prove an integral part in his readjustment.

In additon to these activities, we encouraged John to join an after-school kickball team. His social life expanded, and he became more outgoing and less disturbing because he knew that he was being accepted because of his good behavior. At last he had acceptable outlets for his pent-up energy.

Nothing will change the fact that John was rejected by his parents. He suffered the symptoms of most rejected individuals, behaving in a manner that demanded attention. However, as we were able to help John get started toward a fulfilling life, we are hopeful that he will overcome his problem as completely as possible.

COMMENTS

Teachers and parents can work together to help the child overcome feelings of rejection that may cause disruptive behavior. In chatting with John's grandmother, for example, I was able to learn a lot about him, and together, we worked out a program to help solve his problems.

A child's family situation cannot be left behind him at home. He takes his fears and frustrations to school with him every day. Tragedy or unhappiness at home, and other unpleasant situations in the child's life, cannot be turned off when he enters a school building. An unhappy child almost always behaves differently than a happy one.

A boy rejected by his father, for instance, needs to find acceptance elsewhere. If not, he may strike out in any way he can to get attention. Sometimes that attention comes in the form of punishment for misdeeds. By behaving in a naughty way, he gets someone to notice him. He is no longer being ignored or rejected. A spanking is often just as desirable to a rejected child as a pat on the head, for it tells him that at least someone is paying attention to him in some way. In this sense, we may say that John probably misbehaved on the bus purposely, so that the bus driver would pay attention to him and, in the manner of a correcting father, punish him.

Therefore, a wise adult who sees a child behave in this manner will direct the child toward acceptable goals. We gave John the guidance that got him started toward a more satisfactory way of life. He was introduced to adult males who became substitute father-figures. While none of them could ever take the place of his real father, each performed the function of a father much better than his biological father did.

We encouraged John to join a boys' club. He began to enjoy boys' activities, which were outlets for his tremendous energy. Boys his age are bundles of energy mainly because they are growing so rapidly and taking in great quantities of energy-creating food. Their reactions are lightning swift, and only by playing with others having similar abilities can they really find true companionship.

Most important perhaps is the fact that we made it possible for John to do what he liked. This led to his beginning to enjoy related activities. And because he liked camping, he was willing to read books about campers, thus triggering an overall improvement in his reading skills. He gradually became a well-rounded boy with many interests and friends.

Not all children like to do the same things at any given age, because liking depends upon background and experience. A teacher, therefore, has to make an effort to know the child's preferred activities. If these are socially acceptable and can be engaged in within reason, it is generally advisable to help bring them about.

Parents and guardians must show that they care for their children. Some adults feel that providing material comforts and luxuries is suffcent evidence of love, but children need real care—they need a combination guardian, nursemaid, policeman, judge, counselor, confidant and guide.

A child needs to feel wanted by an understanding, reliable adult. A child needs to be accepted, not rejected, and to know that whatever he does, he can appeal to someone who will understand him and help him toward the life ahead of him. In this respect, teachers, as well as parents, are urgently needed by the child.

——— RECOMMENDED READING

Becker, Wesley C. *Parents Are Teachers*. (A Child Management Program). Champaign, Ill.: Research Press Co., 1971.
Biller, Henry B. *Father, Child and Sex Roles*. Lexington, Mass.: Lexington Books, 1971.
———. *Paternal Deprivation*. Lexington, Mass.: Lexington Books, 1974.
Green, Maureen. *Fathering*. New York: McGraw-Hill, 1976.
Moriarity, David M. *The Loss of Loved Ones*. Springfield, Ill.: C.C. Thomas, 1967.
Stuart, Irving R. *Children of Separation and Divorce*. New York: Grossman Publishers, Inc., 1972.

chapter 14

Karen
(A PROBLEM OF MORALITY)

On the first day of school, a little girl became upset when she could not find her pencil. She described it for her classmates. It was a special one, with a big pink rose on its tip. Although we searched the classroom as thoroughly as we could, the pencil was nowhere to be found.

All I could do was to reassure the child that we would look again the following morning. When I suggested that she may have *thought* she brought it, the idea was vetoed by several children who claimed to have seen her bring it into the classroom.

On the next day, a girl named Karen began to write with a pencil matching the description of the one that had been lost. It created a flurry of excitement.

"Karen has Linda's pencil!" someone exclaimed.

As Linda had not found her pencil, it seemed an odd coincidence that Karen should have one exactly like it. I knew nothing yet about either of the girls, so I hesitated to make any kind of judgment at that point.

Rather than offend Karen, I called both girls into the corridor for a conference. I asked Linda if that pencil looked something like the one she had lost. She replied that it *was* the one she lost, and she accused Karen of stealing it.

I tried to tell Linda that it is not nice to call someone a thief, but she insisted that Karen had her pencil, regardless of the manner in which she had obtained it.

Karen, however, insisted that the pencil was her own. Both girls seemed to be telling the truth and, as far as I knew, they might have been. It is not impossible for two children to purchase identical objects in stores that feature innumerable gadgets during the opening days of school. What convinced me that this was the case was the way they both looked at me, each with an innocent, sincere expression.

Karen's big blue eyes looked hurt as she said, "My mom bought this for me yesterday afternoon."

"In the variety shop on Maple Street?" I asked, knowing that there was no such store at that location, and thus trying to catch Karen in a lie.

She answered in the affirmative. Perhaps she was confused, I decided, doing my best to believe her. Second grade children sometimes have flights of fancy. They are at an age where they must be directed away from make-believe and introduced to reality.

I pushed Karen further. "It's a pretty pencil. How much was it?" I asked.

Karen did not know, and made a move to enter the classroom, as if she wanted to terminate the interview.

"Wait a minute," I said sharply. Karen hesitated and a guilty look appeared on her face, but I realized the tone of my voice might have frightened her. I reminded myself to use a more neutral tone in the future.

"Maybe Linda can buy one like it, since she hasn't found hers," I suggested. "She has to know how much it costs so she has enough money to buy it."

Karen's expression became belligerent as she said, "Ask her how much hers cost then, 'cause I don't know."

I suggested that we telephone Karen's mother to find out the cost. Karen informed me that her mother was at work and could not be disturbed. When I said I would call her at home in the evening, Karen told me they planned to go out that night. I assured her that we would find out the cost eventually, and we returned to the classroom.

In a short time, I noticed that Karen was using an ordinary pencil, and that the rose pencil was not in sight. After looking around the room as inconspicuously as I could under the circumstances, I noticed the rose pencil in the wastebasket. Rather than make an issue of the matter, I asked a boy to toss a paper into the basket for me. He noticed the pencil and fished it out saying, "Here's Linda's pencil!"

When I glanced toward Karen, I noticed that she was writing furiously, not paying any attention to the proceedings, even

104

though the other children had stopped their work. I could have confronted her openly by insisting that the two pencils be compared and perhaps marked in some way to prevent future mixups. However, I was fairly sure that there was only one pencil, making such a confrontation useless.

In order to prevent the establishment of a precedent, I decided to be more watchful of Karen's behavior. In the weeks that followed, I made a list of all the incidents involving missing objects. They all seemed to be centered about Karen. Whenever someone's lunch money was "lost," that someone invariably sat in Karen's vicinity. When a child found something missing from his coat pocket, it was usaully someone who hung the coat near Karen's in the locker. I, too, was the victim of theft. Some spare dimes disappeared from my desk drawer.

I noticed that Karen made a habit of loitering about my desk on some pretense or another. She waited to have her paper checked, or she asked me an unnecessary question while I was checking another child's paper. Although I never saw her actually take anything, objects were missing right after she had been near my desk.

It may have been a coincidence; yet I know that too many coincidences violate the laws of probability. I felt reasonably sure that Karen was the culprit. Was she aware that she was doing wrong, or was she a kleptomaniac and thus not responsible for her actions? I could not make her miserable by confronting her with accusations. That might have been dangerous for any number of reasons, the main one being that I might have been wrong. Yet, I was convinced that she was stealing. The problem was how to catch her in the act and make her aware that she was doing something wrong.

I set a trap by dropping a dime on the floor in the corner before the children entered the room. Dimes seemed to be of special interest to Karen. She often had several to feed into the vending machine to buy treats for herself and her friends. Since her mother had applied for a free lunch ticket for Karen because of a low income situation, I felt that Karen's possession of dimes was suspicious.

The plan did not work at first, for a boy noticed the dime the moment he entered the room and called our attention to it. I put the dime on my desk and feigned some work. Karen flitted about the room, first to the pencil sharpener, then to the waste-basket, her route taking her invariably past my desk. As carefully as I tried to watch her, I did not see her, or anyone, take the dime, and yet it was gone at the end of the day. I began to think I had been wrong about Karen, that someone else had taken it while I was watching the wrong child.

As the days passed, more and more items were "lost." Whenever someone missed something, I was tempted to make a physical search of all the children. Although this practice usually tends to lower morale and develop distrust among the children, eventually it became necessary.

Angela's bracelet disappeared. She had displayed it earlier in the day, showing us the various charms. Then she had removed it because it was difficult for her to write with the charms dangling down her hand. When she announced that it was gone, we searched the room, but no one could find it. At last I decided upon drastic action. I turned out the lights and told the children I would step into the corridor for one minute. That would enable them to close their eyes while the person who had the bracelet could return it to Angela undetected.

I hoped this would make it easier for a child to return the object, without fear of punishment. When I reentered the room, the bracelet had not been returned. Angela began to cry. It was at that point that I decided to be direct. I asked the entire class to stand and then I asked each child individually if he had seen the bracelet. All replies were negative.

Perhaps, I thought, the culprit was dealing in elementary semantics. I changed the wording to, "Have you seen anyone take Angela's bracelet?" Right after the questioning began, Karen suddenly approached me, hand over her mouth, muttering, "I gotta throw up!"

Whenever this happens, most teachers encourage the child to make a hasty exit to the lavatory. Our room helper followed Karen to assist her and to summon the nurse if necessary.

In a little while, when the bracelet subject had been temporarily dropped, the girls returned to the classroom. Karen appeared pale, and her helper declared, "Yuk!" in a disgusted tone.

Could the questioning have upset Karen to the point of making her ill? Had I been unfair? I had been ready to believe that she was faking illness just to escape an unpleasant situation. However, the tone of her helper's voice made it evident that Karen had actually been sick.

The next day there was an *Out of Order* sign on a booth door in the girls' lavatory. The plumber was summoned to fix a plugged toilet. What he discovered proved enlightening—Angela's bracelet was lodged in the bend of the toilet bowl.

I asked Karen's helper which booth Karen had used. It was the one in which the bracelet had been found. Had Karen flushed the bracelet down the toilet to destroy the evidence? She had appeared relieved after returning to the classroom, but I had attributed that to the fact that she felt better.

The question plagued me. How could she have done such a thing with the helper there? I questioned the helper again. Yes, she had gone to the lavatory, but not into the booth with Karen because the sounds were so "yukky," she said. She waited outside the booth until the water stopped running. Karen had emerged from the booth saying that she felt better and did not need to see the nurse.

It was time, I decided, for Karen to be referred for help. I made appointments with a psychologist and a social worker. When Karen's mother was invited for an interview, she became highly indignant at the inference that her child might be mixed up in anything dishonest. During the interview, the case worker noticed Karen rummaging about in her mother's handbag. Her mother admitted that Karen sometimes "borrowed" things, but it was all right with her as the things were all in the family.

Perhaps, then, it was simply a matter of indulgence at home. Immature children often do not realize they are actually stealing. This is especially true when they are allowed to "take" things in their own home.

A few days later, the case worker surprised me with an astonishing revelation. Karen's mother was a known shoplifter. Records indicated that she had been apprehended more than once while stealing from local department stores. The case worker had gone to the police department where the woman's record was on file.

On a Saturday before one Mother's Day, the mother had been caught passing items to Karen who, in turn, placed them into a large shopping bag. Karen was five years old at the time. Mother and child were taken to the manager's office where the mother pleaded that she "didn't know what came over her." Because it would have meant detaining her in jail over Mother's Day, the manager let her go with a warning. He released her without summoning the police. She promised never to enter the store again, for to do so, the manager told her, would mean immediate release of the store records to the police department.

During the interval which followed, the store relocated in a building across the street from its old location. Evidently, Karen's mother was unaware of the change, for she tried shoplifting merchandise from the "other" store. The house detective took her to the manager's office. He did not recognize her, but when she began to cry, "Please don't make me go to jail just before Christmas!" her tune sounded familiar. He took a good look at her, checked his records and summoned the police. This time she was booked. The sentence was suspended because she was all alone, without a husband and the sole support of her three children.

She did not give up stealing. Her methods displayed a good deal of cunning. On one occasion, she and her two boys entered another store. The older boy loitered about one department, keeping his eye on an expensive item he planned to take. The mother and younger boy rode down the escalator together. When they reached the bottom, the boy pretended to get his hand caught in the railing of the moving escalator. He screamed, and his mother shouted hysterically, the ensuing commotion bringing clerks, section managers and house detectives from all parts of the store. During the flurry of activity, the older boy snatched the item he wanted without detection and walked quickly down a stairway and right out of the store.

Karen's mother was on parole simply because she had to support her children. The children had seen enough to know how to steal. Their mother's attitude had given them the idea that it was all right to steal as long as they did not get caught. Even getting caught was not all that bad, because the mother was still, in essence, "free."

Karen was a bright child who learned fast, but she was learning the wrong things and her sense of values was confused. After a great deal of counseling, Karen's mother agreed to send her sons to a correctional facility for rehabilitation. She also agreed to undergo psychiatric therapy. At the same time, Karen was given professional help by a psychologist. It took much soul-searching before Karen's mother could admit that she needed help. The sympathetic approach made to her by the psychologist did much to convince her that she and her children were in trouble, and that without help, their problem would not be solved.

COMMENTS

True kleptomania is rare. Most people who steal are just plain thieves who want to get something for nothing. They may feel cheated by society and thus think they deserve to get something in return. However, they are aware that they are stealing, even if they do not admit it to others.

Kleptomania, on the other hand, is neurotic behavior. Psychologists consider it an obsessive-compulsive reaction. True kleptomaniacs steal for a variety of reasons. Most of them are unaware of the reasons.

Such kleptomanic stealing can sometimes be interpreted as an act of revenge against various forms of authority. For example, a person may resent his parents' authority. He retaliates by doing something to challenge any kind of authority. He tries to outwit the manager of a store. He attempts to baffle the police, who are the ultimate in authority figures to most people.

Often the person who steals compulsively feels hostile toward standards set by society. He does not realize that his feelings of guilt create a need for punishment. Many shoplifters keep stealing the same kind of items from the same stores over and over again. Their action is done not so much out of stupidity as out of a need to be caught and punished.

In this sense, the person is sending out a distress signal. In the case of Karen's mother, no one heeded her signals before she could be helped. She grew up and continued to behave as she did. Worse, she passed on the behavior to her children.

During analysis, it was learned that Karen's mother had deep psychological problems; we shall not go into them in detail here.

Whether or not Karen's mother was a true kleptomaniac is relatively unimportant to us, for we must deal with the problem regardless of its source. The essential factor in Karen's treatment was the fact that Karen had learned undesirable behavior from her mother. What is more, that behavior was reinforced in the form of rewards. When Karen performed well, the mother she loved gave her the approval she needed. Karen had no father, she lived in an incomplete family situation and she may have felt that she was missing something.

Family background plays a big role in the attitude a child has toward right and wrong. In most instances, the child learns this attitude directly from his parent or parents. Occasionally, he learns it from brothers and sisters, and sometimes from his friends. Young children do not have to be taught to do most things; they commonly imitate those around them.

When the child imitates wrong behavior and is rewarded for doing so, he is probably headed for future trouble. Karen had never really learned the sharp distinction between moral right and wrong, although she was able to understand it when given guidance and counseling.

This distinguishes her from the true kleptomaniac, who is actually so disturbed that he does not realize what he is doing, nor does he possess the ability to grasp the implications of his act.

Punishment and embarrassment are rarely effective in helping such a person as I have shown in Karen's case. Children with similar problems who would exhibit similar behavior are those who tell lies habitually, cheat on tests, or perform any acts which are generally considered wrong by society as a whole.

In Karen's case, I tried to avoid open confrontation. Such situations can lead to hostility of a child toward a teacher, and to feelings of inadequacy and inferiority in the child. At one point, I could not follow my own advice, but, rather, found it necessary to challenge Karen openly. It was not an ideal way to treat the situation. I included this aspect of the case to show you how a person can react when under pressure and in an unusual situation, for which there is no precedent. I hope that you may profit from my experience.

It is important to realize that most young children go through phases when they steal, lie or cheat. They must be taught to change their behavior with patience and kindness, not with threats of punishment. By setting a good example, we can guide them toward acceptable modes of behavior.

Because Karen's case required professional help above and beyond school staff, and because a child with whom you are concerned may need such help, I am listing below some suggestions for obtaining it. Your telephone directory's classified section gives exact names and addresses for the following:

1. Clergy
2. Clinics
3. County Medical Guidance Clinics
4. Family Counselors
5. Family Service Organizations
6. Mental Health Clinics
7. Psychiatric Clinics
8. Psychologists
9. Physicians

——————— RECOMMENDED READING

Kay, William. *Moral Development*. London: Allen & Unwin, 1968.

Klein, Roger D. *Behavior Modification in Classroom Settings*. Springfield, Ill.: C.C. Thomas, 1973.

Moore, Dewey J. *Preventing Misbehavior in Children*. Springfield, Ill.: C.C. Thomas, 1972.

Stumphauzer, Jerome S. *Behavior Therapy with Delinquents*. Springfield, Ill.: C.C. Thomas, 1973.

Walker, Robert N. *Psychology of the Youthful Offender*. Springfield, Ill.: C. C. Thomas, 1973.

chapter 15

Brian
(A PROBLEM OF PERSPECTIVE)

When Brian was assigned to my fourth grade classroom, I accepted him with mixed feelings. His father was the principal of our school, and Brian's previous teachers had been burdened with the problem of pleasing the principal at the expense of dealing fairly with the boy.

Brian was an only child. In addition to the fact that he was the principal's son, his mother had been a teacher at the school, and both parents considered Brian an exceptionally brilliant child. That he was not accomplishing as much as the other children in his class was of little consequence to them. They considered him a "late-blooming child" who would eventually show everyone how intelligent he really was.

In one way I felt privileged to have Brian in my classroom. On the other hand, I knew that I would be under constant scrutiny. Because the boy's previous teachers had given such glowing accounts of his ability, any fair appraisal of his work on my part might be suspect by the doting parents.

Brian's superior air of self-assurance caught my attention at once. There was no doubt that he considered himself important in the school. The other children disliked him, although they seemed to envy him because he was always favored by the faculty.

Whenever I introduced a subject for study, Brian announced that he already knew all about it. Evidently the curriculum was discussed at home within his hearing. I suspected that his father used Brian as a sort of "guinea pig" in an effort to discover subjects most interesting to children. Then he suggested that those subjects be included in the curriculum.

I had to be careful about the way I reacted to Brian. It was difficult for me to be objective when he mentioned that teachers had to do things a certain way because his father said so. It was not easy to maintain an air of authority in his presence.

Perhaps the word *authority* is a poor choice here. Most teachers try to conduct their classes by being guides rather than authoritative, autocratic figures. But I felt that I was being made subordinate to the boy.

Whenever I corrected a child, it was likely that the child would complain to Brian. It was common knowledge that Brian would "go over my head" and report instances of what he considered unfairness to his father.

It is customary for the principal to observe each classroom teacher at intervals. While Brian was in my room, his father dropped in daily. At those times, Brian conferred with him about their lunch plans or after-school activities. Whether or not the principal expected me to criticize Brian for this behavior I could only guess. From his annoyed attitude during the one time I commented upon it, I assumed that he regarded his son as a privileged member of the group.

The other children noticed Brian's freedom and took advantage of my good nature. They walked about the room during lessons, and talked while I tried to teach. It was apparent that their respect for me was being undermined by the principal's son. I knew that I must do something before the entire class got out of control.

Brian seldom finished his assignments. Despite the fact that we had a rule about unfinished work, that is, it had to be done for homework and returned the following day, Brian never brought any homework papers to school. I questioned him about it. He explained in a patronizing manner that his mother was a teacher who always corrected his papers and found them perfect. Yet, whenever we had a test, Brian's results were far from good. He had been a straight *A* student in his first three grades. Would I be considered a poor teacher if I suddenly began giving him the *D* grades he deserved?

I tried to discuss Brian's work with his father. To my consternation, the principal always dismissed the topic. His usual comment was, "Report cards and grades will soon be things of the past. Tests prove nothing. Parent-teacher conferences will be popular. We want to be progressive." He did not seem to understand that I was attempting to have a parent-teacher conference with him.

In January, Brian was absent for a prolonged interval with a severe case of flu. While he was gone, the climate in the classroom changed so dramatically that I was convinced it must be attributed to Brian's absence. The children became more attentive, interested in their work and more respectful toward me. They no longer presented me with constant challenges that seemed to undermine my position as their leader. Teaching became a pleasure once more.

It occurred to me then that Brian was a problem child who needed help. How could this be made apparent to his parents, particularly to his father? How could Brian be helped by me and by his classmates?

I decided that I must begin to treat him like any other child. Firmness, fairness and true interest in his welfare became my plan for dealing with him. To prepare for this goal, I began an informal campaign to make him popular with the children, or if not popular, at least in a position to be understood. We made "get well" cards for him. When someone suggested sending them to the office for his father to take home, I suggested that Brian might like to get some mail.

It was our custom to have one of the children deliver cards in person, or, if the absentee had something contagious or infectious, for the class as a whole to walk to the nearby post office to mail the cards in one large envelope. The children were surprised that Brian was to receive the standard treatment. Mixed with their surprise, I sensed a keen interest in the outcome of the act.

Did they think the principal would be offended that his son had been treated like all the other children? Did they want to know if this would influence my relationship with Brian? Did I imagine this, and give the children credit for thoughts and speculations far beyond their years?

One of the children justified my suspicious thoughts. A boy asked, "Do you think the principal will be sore?"

The children began to wonder why the principal no longer made daily visits to the classroom. They began to realize that

Brian might have been responsible for all the attention we got from his father. The last thing I wanted to do was undermine the children's respect for the principal. Also, I did not want to be on unfriendly terms with the principal's son.

It was a good opportunity to discuss the children's feelings toward Brian and his position in their group. We began by talking about parents' occupations. Eventually, the subject of having a principal for a father arose. Some of the children thought it would be good; that it would insure passing grades, and that they would not have to fear a trip to the principal's office.

Some, on the other hand, thought it would be awful. They did not like the idea of listening to school talk at home. A few objected to being under constant supervision by a principal.

They began to see Brian in a different light. Some envied him, others pitied him; all, however, began to have changed feelings toward him. Perhaps their feelings would become evident when he returned. It was a hopeful prospect.

On the day he returned, we discussed the progress we had made during the first semester and what we hoped to accomplish in the second. The boys and girls began to formulate a set of rules that they thought would be good to follow. Brian, of course, quoted his father. Unlike instances in the past, many of his remarks were ignored.

He sulked at first. When his face lit up in a malicious smirk, it became obvious that he planned to inform his father about the activities in the classroom. He began to radiate some of the old confidence. What he did not know was that I, too, had gained some much-needed confidence. I had failed in the past to regard him as one of the children. Now that I had decided to change, my courage increased.

On that first day back, Brian failed to complete his assignments, claiming to feel tired. Whenever a child returns after a prolonged or severe illness, most teachers allow recovery time. We understand that the child needs to regain his strength. Thus, I treated Brian leniently for a few days. On the fifth day, however, he was strong enough for a boisterous gym period, so I insisted that he complete his work.

He said that he would finish it at home. I had anticipated this and was prepared. Duplicated notes were distributed to all of the children, reminding them that homework papers must be looked at and signed by at least one parent in order to be accepted by me.

On the following day, the prinicipal approached me in the teachers' lunchroom. In his hand was Brian's paper. He asked why Brian had never received homework papers before, and why Brian was so poor in math. Was it because he had been absent?

It was evident that Brian had never taken any of his incomplete papers home. His mother had not seen them as he had claimed. When I informed Brian's father that his son had needed homework all year, but neglected to do the work at home, he refused to believe that Brian was capable of such behavior. The previous night had been the first time he or his wife had seen any paper. Brian's mother had assumed that he was doing too well to make homework necessary. It was obvious that Brian had not told his parents the truth, evidence that he may not have wanted them to know that he was unable to handle the work, afraid to admit that fact to parents who took it for granted that he could do it.

His parents expected too much of him, and Brian felt the need to live up to those expectations. Because he was unable to do so, he used the most readily available "crutch"— the superiority of his father's position. He sensed that any teacher would probably treat him as his first teacher had, because he was his father's son. Thus the habit of using his father to escape difficult work evolved. It was a typical pattern of simple, learned behavior.

I decided that it was time for that pattern to be changed. Fundamentally, the principal seemed to be a fair-minded person. In dealing with most problems he was quite objective. It was only in matters relating to his son that he lost his usually realistic perspective.

When I persisted in my statements about Brian's work, he began to understand the situation sooner than I had hoped he would. He asked to see Brian in his office the next afternoon.

At two o'clock on the following day, I called Brian to my desk and told him quietly that the principal wanted to see him in his office. At first Brian protested, explaining that he would be home in a short time and could talk to his father then. I repeated in a quiet but firm tone that it was not his father, but the principal, who wished to interview him.

Brian looked at me with a slight trace of alarm in his eyes. Then, after more hesitation, he went out.

In about a half hour, Brian returned, handed me a note and went to his desk. As it was almost dismissal time, the children were playing a game, their reward for completing their work. Brian did not join them, but rather sulked, red faced, at his desk.

Because he had not finished his work, I handed him a homework paper on his way out of the room. The other children seemed to sense that Brian was at last being treated as one of them. None of them actually questioned his absence from the room, and I doubt that he told them he had been to the principal's office.

The next day Brian turned in his homework. The paper was signed by his mother and countersigned by his father. I told him it was a good paper and that I hoped he would continue to do good work. He looked as though he anticipated further comment from me. I simply smiled. His work that day was satisfactory and he did not show off in front of others. Instead of sitting there with a knowing smirk on his face, he asked intelligent questions. That smirk, I knew now, probably covered his lack of ability to grasp many concepts. It was a defense mechanism that had been operating for him during most of his school years.

Now he was beginning to function without it. His mind was opening up to learning instead of "knowing it all." Thanks to his father's treatment of him, Brian became one of the kids. His work was not superior, but began to show daily improvement because of his dedicated application. The principal's estimation of me as a teacher did not diminish, as I had mistakenly feared, and I had an added respect for him as an administrator and, especially, as a parent.

COMMENTS

I have used the example of a principal's child. It could have been the daughter of the president of the United States or a child of a fellow teacher or an influential neighbor. It is essential that such a child be treated exactly the same as the other children. And it is very important that the relationship between you and the child be established on your first encounter with the child. Getting started in the wrong way can lead to serious trouble.

I realize that it may be difficult to handle such a situation in the way I suggest, and, in some instances, almost impossible. Every parent who is also an intelligent leader may feel that his child is exceptional. There are many generalizations made, such as "Teachers have the best kids to teach," or, "Teachers have the worst kids to teach." Generalizations are not usually valid. Many teachers I know regard their own children as superior, or as outstanding scholars, while many are realistic enough to admit the truth if their children are just "average" students.

Of course, educators often make good parents because they have access to the means to help their children advance, or they apply those means in the most effective way. In my own experience, I have found that many parents, who are also educators, make exaggerated claims about their children's abilities more as a means to prove that they themselves are exceptional parents than to prove their children are exceptional. Teachers must always beware of too readily believing the claims of previous teachers or influential parents about a child.

Accountability is becoming an important aspect of teaching. Some teachers may feel that their competence is being challenged if they cannot, in fact, work wonders with a so-called "wonder child." This is especially true if the preceding teacher has claimed unusual success with the child.

Good teachers, as well as concerned parents, try to avoid open conflict. They try to be aware of playing the group against the child. Such a child is in an awkward position among his peers in the first place. Teachers and parents can help the child gain and maintain the proper perspective on his place in the classroom.

We should do everything in our power to help the child develop habits and attitudes that will lead to his classmates' acceptance of him. It is important to be direct and yet discreet. An example of discretion in Brian's case was giving *all* of the children homework notes rather than singling out Brian and thereby drawing attention to him. Discretion was also shown in calling him aside to tell him to go to the principal's office rather than announcing it in front of his classmates. It was also required in telling Brian's father tactfully what he needed to know. Brian's father showed discretion in the way he subsequently handled his son. He still visited the classroom, but showed interest in all of the children, and his visits gradually tapered off until they occurred only on special occasions.

We should try to realize the problems faced by the child of an exceptional person. A teacher could easily resent such a child. The child's classmates could easily envy him. The parents could be overly sensitive. These are enormous problems for a child to cope with.

This chapter has been written from a teacher's point of view. Yet I feel that parents as well as teachers may gain appreciation of the problems encountered by a child in a situation similar to Brian's. And, they may also apprehend the problems faced by parents and teachers in such situations. They should help all concerned to help the child which is, after all, the goal.

———— RECOMMENDED READING

Elich, Peter J. *The Modification of Children's Judgements*. Ann Arbor: University of Oregon Press, 1962.
Grey, Loren. *Discipline Without Fear*. New York: Hawthorn Books, 1974.
————. *Discipline Without Tyranny*. New York: Hawthorn Books, 1972.
Madsen, Clifford K. *Parents Children Discipline*. Boston: Allyn & Bacon, Inc., 1972.

chapter 16

Melissa
(A PROBLEM OF PARENTAL HANDICAP)

Melissa rarely stopped talking. From the moment she entered my third grade classroom in the morning until dismissal time, she carried on incessant conversation. The conversation was usually onesided, as the other children paid little attention to her. If no one listened, she talked to herself, or sometimes hummed. She did not talk loudly enough to disturb anyone, but her preoccupation with talking made it difficult for her to listen to directions. Consequently, her work began to fall behind that of the others in her group.

My admonitions about listening were ignored by Melissa, who seemed to have no desire to pay attention. When I discussed this with her second grade teacher, I learned that Melissa had been disruptive also during the previous year. The disruption had not been considered serious enough to warrant a parental conference, although if it had, the parents would probably not have cooperated. The former teacher, as well as the school office staff, considered Melissa's parents uninterested in their daughter or in her school activities.

Ours is a school which sends out report cards at periodic intervals. Parent-teacher conferences are matters of routine, but I thought it was time to summon one or both of Melissa's parents to a meeting. When I telephoned the number that appeared on Melissa's record card, a neighbor answered. The neighbor, who lived in the apartment next to Melissa's, informed me that both of Melissa's parents were deaf-mutes, whose custom it was to receive messages relayed by the neighbor. I asked the neighbor to communicate to the parents that I would send a note home with Melissa about her inadequate school work. The moment I put down the telephone, I realized that I had been indiscreet in giving information to a neighbor about a child's work. Nevertheless, from the way in which the neighbor spoke, she seemed to know all of the family's business and had expressed a keen interest in Melissa.

I wondered why the parents' handicaps had not been noted on Melissa's school record card. She had been in our school for four years. How had she been enrolled? Would not the office clerk have noticed a parent who was unable to talk or hear? I also wondered why Melissa had never mentioned these things herself. Was she ashamed of her parents? Often such differences from others make a child feel inferior. It was also curious that none of the other children who lived near Melissa seemed to know about her parents.

In answer to my note, a long letter arrived, explaining that the parents would be willing to meet me in private, provided that Melissa was allowed to be present as an interpreter. It was interesting to speculate how an eight-year-old girl would convey her parents' thoughts to me. When all of us were seated in a conference room, I was pleasantly surprised. Melissa became the focal point of the meeting, communicating with her parents in the approved sign language for deaf-mutes, and then telling me verbally what they "told" her.

We learned a great deal during that interview. Near its termination, the parents expressed their wish for Melissa to leave. With some misgivings, I sent her back to the classroom, wondering at the same time, how I would be able to understand them or make myself clear to them.

After Melissa left, her father produced a small paper pad and pencil. He began to dash off sentences for me to read, and I was asked to write answers. Her parents were at an advantage, as they were accustomed to writing their thoughts quickly and reading the replies almost instantaneously. I had been accustomed to the "handicap" of speech and hearing! After a little practice, I began to communicate with them more easily, and we worked out a temporary solution to Melissa's dilemma. The main problem seemed to be the reluctance of Melissa and her parents to have their handicap known. That is why none of Melissa's little friends were aware of the situation. They assumed that the neighbor lady whom they saw with Melissa in the supermarket was her mother. Melissa chose to allow them to believe this rather than admit that her parents were different.

A subject in our curriculum seemed well adapted to bringing Melissa out of her shell. We began a unit on communication, studying the telephone, television, newspaper, books and magazines. We discussed how all of these were considered means of communicating thoughts and ideas from one person to the next. We branched out to more subtle ways, such as Indian smoke signals, and the hand signals given by a symphony conductor to communicate with various musicians during a performance.

We took a bus trip to the local Coast Guard Station where we were shown signals in which colored code flags were used to spell out words. Upon our return to the classroom we began to make paper flags in the style of the international code signal flags. Some of the children devised secret systems of their own, by which they sent messages back and forth across the room.

In an off-hand manner, I inquired if anyone knew of any different ways to communicate with people. To my delight, Melissa, carried away by the fun of the project, volunteered the information that she always "talked" to her parents in sign language. When the other children asked her why, she sensed their genuine interest, and, more important, she wished to impress them by knowing something they did not know, so she told them of her parents' condition.

She further amazed the children with a series of gestures that made sense to them and which they wanted to learn immediately. Soon they knew how to give the signs for such sentences as, "May I leave the room?" or "I need a drink of water, for I have hiccoughs."

We set aside a period of time each day after that in which we encouraged Melissa to teach the signs. It gave Melissa a necessary outlet for her need to communicate. She always began by talking, to explain what the signals meant, and then commenced to show us the graceful hand movements. Soon the entire class was "talking" in sign language much of the time—it was the quietest class I have ever taught!

The climax of Melissa's instruction was a special presentation of the song "Raindrops Keep Fallin' on My Head" in sign language. During the school's spring program, most of the children either talked or sang. When it was our turn, we played the record of the raindrop song, while the children lined up and demonstrated the words in sign language in front of a spell-bound audience. Among those who came to see the program were Melissa's parents, who were of course delighted to understand some of the performance so well.

After that, Melissa's parents began to attend parent-teacher meetings. Other parents, who had learned of their condition, felt less awkward about them because of their children's ability to communicate with them. Some of the parents learned from their children how to say "Hello" in sign language, making Melissa's parents feel welcome.

Their changed attitude, along with Melissa's outlet for expressing herself, helped the family's entire situation. Melissa no longer needed to talk incessantly, nor was she embarrassed by her parents; rather she became proud of them and of her own accomplishments.

COMMENTS

Most children have a strong need to conform, so a child with handicapped parents may feel inferior when he realizes that his parents are different from the parents of other children. The child is unhappy and feels shame and embarrassment because of his parents, but serious problems lie ahead if he tries to cover up the reality of his situation and pretend that it is completely normal. The suppression of emotions can cause real suffering, as in Melissa's case.

Handicaps may be of a physical nature, such as deafness, blindness or lameness. They may be emotionally induced, such as many cases of alcoholism, drug addiction or mental disease. A colleague of mine mentioned how sensitive a student of his was because her parents were fat, and another was ashamed of his mother's protruding teeth. Some children try to hide the fact that their parents cannot read or write. Often the handicap will be in the parent's vocation. In a group where most of the parents are professional people, a child whose father is an untrained laborer may be ashamed of the fact.

By having both parents handicapped, Melissa was at a disadvantage. It was obvious that her compulsion to voice her thoughts by incessant talking in school was caused by the fact that she had no opportunity to "talk" to her parents at home. It must have been frustrating for her to live two lives: At home she could make as much noise as she wanted, for no one heard; while at school, she was asked to be quiet. Because she needed experience in communicating with normal persons, and because that experience could not be attained at home, she compensated by talking more than usual in school.

When encouraged to teach her classmates something they were eager to learn, Melissa profited in two ways. She overcame her embarrassment over her parents' handicap, and she assumed an important role in her own group. This built up her confidence as well as providing her with the opportunity to talk all she wanted.

Melissa's parents profited, too, by being accepted by other parents. The children who had been in contact with Melissa educated their parents by taking home what they had learned from her. We adults can learn much from children if we give them the opportunity to teach us.

Handicaps need not be limitations to learning but, on the contrary, they can open new vistas of unlimited proportions. We should be alert to ways of promoting interest and directing a child's behavior toward positive goals. In this way, such a child's problem can be handled constructively and creatively.

It was unfortunate that Melissa's problem went so long before being detected. The fact that her parents were deaf-mutes was not recorded on her school documents. This was partly the fault of her parents, who undoubtedly thought they were doing her a favor by having some normal person attend to her registration at school.

The school was partly to blame, in that the clerk who admitted Melissa did not take note of the name of the person who signed the child'd papers. Such an occurrence is rare, but when it happens, it can, as in Melissa's case, be serious. Had the secret been kept longer, Melissa might have been considered a disruptive child, and her education would have suffered along with her personality.

The information about Melissa's parents was added to her

permanet record card, under the heading *Physical Limitations*. While it was not actually a limitation of Melissa's, it certainly had to be considered a limiting factor in the child's behavior. Her home life was indeed different from the average child's. The notation on her card would help explain her behavior to future teachers.

———— RECOMMENDED READING

Birdwhistell, Roy L. *Kinesics and Context*. Philadelphia: University of Philadelphia Press, 1970.

Dale, Dion M. *Deaf Children at Home and at School*. Springfield, Ill.: C.C. Thomas, 1967.

Davis, Flora. *Inside Intuition–What we know about Nonverbal Communication*. New York: McGraw-Hill Book Co., 1973.

Harrison, Randall. *Beyond Words*. Englewood Cliffs, N.J.: Prentice Hall, Inc., 1974.

Mehrabian, Albert. *Silent Messages*. Belmont, Cal.: Wadsworth Publishing Co., 1971.

Wolff, Sydney, *Games Without Words*. Springfield, Ill.: C.C. Thomas, 1974.

chapter 17

Robert
(A PROBLEM OF JUDGMENT)

Robert was an intelligent boy, keenly observant and interested in many subjects. However, at study work time, he became restless and refused to do his assignments. Instead, he wandered around the classroom, talked loudly or sometimes shouted at passers-by.

Efforts to encourage him to participate in the work failed. He had no interest in the usual rewards for good work, which consisted of receiving a privilege, or planning a special project. The only reward that Robert responded to was being paid in cash.

When asked to finish his work, Robert stated flatly that he would do it only for a sum of money.

"People don't work for nothing," he said. "Why should I, just because I'm a kid?"

Robert did not do his homework in the usual way. His father allowed him to borrow an electronic calculator to do his math homework. He reflected his father's philosophy by saying, "As long as there's an easy way to do something with a machine, why do it the hard way?"

I suppose the boy had a point, but, by working with an adding machine, Robert did not gain understanding of the mathematical concepts behind its operations. Furthermore, he carried his philosophy into all subject areas. When he was asked to write a letter to a child in another classroom, he refused, saying, "When I grow up, I'll have a dictating machine to use, and a secretary to write my letters for me, so why all the fuss about learning to write silly old letters?"

Robert seemed to have an answer for everything. His work began to drop far below the level of his grade. Because I knew he was capable of doing the work if he tried, I delivered an ultimatum. Unless he completed a study work paper, he would be suspended from school. I knew this would displease his father, who valued an education.

Robert realized it, too; right after that he began to hand in papers. In a few days, however, something about the papers aroused my suspicion. They did not seem to be written in Robert's handwriting.

I watched him closely and discovered that a friend of his actually did the work for him. Eventually, I found out, in a roundabout way, that Robert gave the friend 50 cents every time he did Robert's work. Although Robert was an affluent boy and could well afford to pay such a sum, it was undesirable for him to do so for two reasons: First, his work was suffering, and he was in danger of failing. Second, he was doing something underhanded.

What kind of incentive would motivate Robert to the same extent that other, less complicated things motivated most students? I tried to discover such an incentive as the weeks went by. The paid-for papers with Robert's name continued to be handed in daily, while I pretended to be deceived by the scheme and graded the papers as though they were Robert's. I knew it was useless to confront Robert directly, as he would have an excuse ready. It was necessary to wait until I could find something to arouse his interest and thus change the situation.

On the day that report cards were to be distributed, Robert brought me an expensive gift, an obvious bribe. He undoubtedly believed that the gesture would induce me to give him good grades. It showed how childish he actually was, for he momentarily forgot that he had fooled me into thinking he had submitted the work papers and thus was deserving of good grades. I considered failing him just to teach him a lesson, but I had nothing to substantiate failing marks. He did, after all, give me papers with his name on them, papers which I had graded with passing marks. It seemed as though I had fallen into my own trap.

The other children responded favorably to positive remarks such as, "Wonderful paper!" or "Keep up the good work!" I could think of nothing to say to Robert that would elicit a positive response from him.

One day, someone asked if we might play Bingo. We obtained some cards and used seashells as markers. The prizes consisted of things such as lollipops, baseball cards or small charms. The children were allowed to play only when their day's work was completed.

Robert showed interest in the game until he learned that it would not be played for a big cash prize. He even suggested that each child donate some money, in the manner of a pool or lottery, to make up the prize. When he discovered that would be impossible, he refused to play. While the others played, he wandered about the room, sometimes "accidentally" bumping their cards and upsetting their games until his behavior began to spoil the game for everyone.

At library time, Robert refused to take out library books. While some children had a library card and used the public library, making it unnecessary to use the school facilities, this was not the case with Robert. He claimed that his father bought him any books he wanted and further stated that the books at school were "silly."

Because he enjoyed showing off his possessions, I asked him to bring some of his own books to share with the class. Most of the books he brought were involved with trains. Whenever he showed such a book, I could see his keen interest in trains, so I tried a new approach with him.

My grandfather had been a railroad man who, long ago, had built a wooden miniature train, consisting of a hand-carved locomotive and cars. While all of the moving parts were still intact, some needed to be adjusted or repaired slightly. I brought the train to school, placed it on the activity table, and announced that any interested children might fix it up as a special project. It was generally understood that only those children who finished their work could engage in special activities.

During study time, I noticed Robert loitering about the activity table. As usual, he had not even started his assignment, but was evidently waiting for his friend to finish his own work before beginning the additional paper. I sent his friend to another classroom which was taught by a teacher with whom I had discussed Robert. As previously arranged, she kept the boy occupied for the duration of our study time.

In this way, Robert had no opportunity to have his work

done for him. When I reminded him about the rules for working on special projects, he began to sulk. At last, when his friend continued to be absent from the room, Robert sat down and started his assignment.

I made it a point to approach Robert's desk at frequent intervals while he worked. This showed him that I was interested in his completion of the assignment. When I commented, "Your writing looks different today," his face flushed. He continued to write, though, until the paper was finished, and when it was checked, he began to work on the special project.

The project lasted several weeks. At the end of that time, I hoped that Robert would be sufficiently interested in work to continue doing his own assignments. As soon as the train was completely renovated and on display, though, he began paying his friend to do his work once again.

Keeping up with Robert's interests in order to motivate him was a most difficult task. I must admit that I was a failure. He barely passed his final exams. In the following grade, the teacher had the same trouble with him.

COMMENTS

Robert's case was not as hopeless as I have made it seem. I purposely ended it at this point because most teachers come to the end of a school year and then have little or no opportunity to continue working with a certain child. They often do not have time or opportunity to continue any interest in the children who have passed through their rooms. Thus, other teachers or parents who may be tempted to criticize a teacher's failure to help a child may be doing so unjustly.

The fact of the matter is that time ran out for Robert and me. All I could do was make notations on his record card and hope that his next teacher, in whatever school he attended, would have better luck in getting him interested in work.

It took several years before Robert was actually helped. I had been disappointed in myself for not confronting him openly. That, however, did not work when tried by some of his later teachers, but rather made him, and his father, behave in a hostile manner. Those teachers were considered "unfair" by his father, a man who was accustomed to buying his way in the world and ordering others around.

The boy's home situation was obviously causing his attitudes. Robert was affluent enough to buy what he needed, namely, "hired help." His father was manager of a big business and, as such, he made the adding machines and other office equipment available to Robert to assist him in his schoolwork.

Most teachers encourage parental interest in their children's work. Robert's father, however, did not help him directly; he was too busy to work with the boy personally.

Robert considered his father's methods far superior to those of his teachers. I learned later that it is wise to interview a parent and discuss the home attitudes which might be influencing the child. An upper grade teacher at last found a way to reach Robert *and* his father as a result of doing this. It was done without undermining Robert's respect for his father or his teachers. Because Robert thought so much of his father, it was, indeed, a tricky feat.

Four years after Robert was in my classroom, his teacher had a conference with his father. They discussed, as other teachers had, Robert's attitudes and how they were affecting the boy's work. The fact that Robert was the son of an influential businessman in the community became the important factor and enabled the teacher to ask for the father's help.

Robert's father, an extremely efficient man, visited Robert's class and explained the principles of company management. These were then compared with classroom management. As an incentive, Robert was asked to "manage" the classroom as a reward for good work. Thus, Robert, following in his father's footsteps, was made general manager of the classroom, maintaining a position much like his father's.

Because Robert was intelligent and grasped concepts quickly when he wanted to do so, he was asked to supervise the work of slower children and offer his help. In order to help them, of course, he needed to understand the assignments and be capable of completing them himself. That meant he had to work up to par.

When the teacher discussed goals with Robert's father, both

men decided that Robert's goals should become less merce-nary. In fact, Robert's father was embarrassed to admit that he had instilled such attitudes in his son. He was big enough to realize his error, and, at home, he began to reward Robert with less mercenary things.

One rule was made strict—in order to function in a supervi-sory capacity, Robert had to complete his own work first. At last a good way to motivate him was found. Robert was a born leader. His experience at home, with a father who was a "boss," reinforced this aspect of his personality. He was al-lowed to be a leader whenever he behaved in an approved manner.

In this way, his behavior was modified to his advantage. He offered his services to others and in return he was respected and admired. He learned that these commodities cannot be bought with money, but must be earned. He learned that he was important, not for his money or for his father's influential position, but for himself and the services he could render to others. This filled a great need.

Robert's story brings into focus the point, essential for teach-ers to note, that parents who are affluent may be tempted to buy their child's respect or admiration. They often do not real-ize that children need basic values which cannot be purchased. A child needs his parents' attention and time. If a parent spends more time with a child, the child's attitudes can be shaped in a desirable way. The child can learn to give of him-self, to cooperate with others and to share in mutual under-takings.

Of course, most parents wish their children to have more than they themselves had. Yet we often see many young people from well-to-do homes rebel against the very society in which they find themselves. Each generation needs to work out its problems in its own way. To carry the burden of an "inheri-tance of attitudes" often makes it impossible to become an in-dividual who is capable of being himself. That quality seems to gain more respect than most others. If an individual is re-spected by others, his self-esteem is elevated. Usually he is a better adjusted person, with fewer problems.

Fortunately Robert was reached in time, both by his father in the home situation and by a teacher. It took cooperation on the part of everyone concerned. Most of all, it required an understanding of the kind of distress signal Robert was sending out. Once that signal was detected, no miraculous "remedy" was put into action. It took years of speculation and search until an effective remedy was tried and found successful.

All problem cases are not simple cause-and-effect situations. It is not merely a matter of noting a signal and putting into action an effective "cure." That approach would oversimplify matters and be completely unrealistic. All we can do is to try every known method of solving the problem and hope for success. Willingness to keep trying is an important factor.

——— RECOMMENDED READING

Homme, Lloyd E. et al. *How to Use Contingency Contracting in the Classroom*. Champaign, Ill.: Research Press, 1970.

Logan, Frank Anderson. *Reward and Punishment*. Boston: Allyn & Bacon, Inc., 1965.

Neisworth, John T. et al. *Student Motivation and Classroom Management*. Lemont, Pa.: Behavior Technics, 1973.

Plowman, Paul Dearborne. *Behavioral Objectives*. Chicago: Science Research Associates, 1971.

chapter 18

Deborah
(A PROBLEM OF UNREASONABLE FEAR)

Deborah was terrified of strange dogs. She was so afraid of them that she could not walk to school alone, but had to be accompanied by her mother in case she was confronted by a stray dog, in which case she would go into hysterics.

Deborah's fear seemed absurd to her parents who could think of no reason for her to get upset by dogs. She had never been bitten or otherwise attacked by one. Her family owned a large, friendly German shepherd and assumed that this pet would help Deborah see that dogs in general need not be feared. Nevertheless, Deobrah became panic-stricken at the sight of a strange dog even when the dog was behind a fence and her parents were present to protect her.

During a talk with Deborah's mother, I suggested that the school psychologist might be able to offer some help. Despite the fact that the psychologist usually handles problems directly related to a child's school behavior, I believed that he should investigate a problem that was serious enough to affect Deborah's behavior so drastically and would certainly influence her school performance.

After preliminary tests, the psychologist decided that Deborah needed psychiatric help. As Deborah's teacher, I was asked to assist in the process of determining why Deborah reacted as she did toward strange dogs. During the process of Deborah's case study, I learned a great deal about the ways in which fears develop, and also various ways in which trained individuals can investigate a person's background to determine possible causes of fears.

Deborah's hysteria whenever she saw a strange dog was her distress signal. What was it about the dogs that set her off, and why did she react in that manner? The psychologist, psychiatrist, Deborah's parents and I worked together in an attempt to discover something in Deborah's past that was responsible for her current behavior.

We established the fact that she had never been bitten by a dog. That, or any kind of attack, would have been a simple reason for her to be afraid of dogs. Many fears are developed in that way; one frightening experience is enough to cause lifetime fear. A child who once almost drowns, for example, may be forever afraid of going into the water. Further, he may generalize the fear and dislike getting his face washed, or even watching fish in an aquarium. If he is put under stress at a future time, he might become violent and smash a fishbowl for no "apparent" reason.

Obviously, something other than a bad experience with a dog made Deborah behave the way she did. In the search into her past, knowledge of child behavior was an important factor. For example, I found out that up to the age of four, children's fears are generally associated with concrete objects. Had Deborah been frightened by *any* animal when she was very young?

That, of course, was impossible to ascertain. A toy dog, or any stuffed, furry animal, might have been innocently thrust in her face by an older child, at a moment when she was separated from her mother. Any supposed threat to one's life or health can create a feeling of fear.

Sometimes even more powerful than threat to life or well-being is the threat to self-esteem. Could Deborah, then, have been anxious about something that made her feel insignificant? Because children need attention, perhaps she was not getting enough from her parents, and her hysterics provided a way to do so. If that were the case, why did she act that way only in the presence of strange dogs?

We know that children often acquire their fears from adults whom they love and admire. It is their way of learning to imitate the adult way of life. When her parents tried to recall whether they or any relatives had encountered a mean dog in the past, one of her aunts remembered having talked about a frightening experience she had had.

"I can't recall mentioning it in front of Debbie," she said, "but she may have overheard."

"I was holding the baby in my arms," she went on, recalling how frightened she had been while baby-sitting for a neighbor. "All of a sudden a Boston terrier jumped out of nowhere and grabbed the baby's leg. That awful dog just held on and wouldn't let go. Almost chewed the leg off."

The psychiatrist decided against questioning Deborah about the incident, because if she had not heard of her aunt's experience in the past, hearing it now might make her more frightened than she was already.

If Deborah had not learned her fear from mimicking an adult, she might have copied a playmate whom she admired, as six-year-old children often do. However, no one could suggest any child of Deborah's acquaintance who feared dogs.

We inquired about the kind of stories Deborah was told, which books were read to her, what television shows she was allowed to watch, and what the adults in her household talked about. A series of articles, or a television documentary about a rabid dog might be sensational enough to sell newspapers or promote a product advertised by a television commercial. Adults discussing sensational events—a story about a rabid dog, for example—might inject enough concern into their voices to scare a child.

A healthy respect for potentially dangerous situations is wise, for it is more sensible to be discreet than reckless, but many adults overdo their warnings; their facial expressions indicating disaster, their tone of voice suggesting doom. Children, sensitive to body language, sometimes take such warnings too seriously, generalizing the situation with the result that, instead of fearing hostile, diseased or aggressive animals, they learn to be afraid of any strange animal.

Thus, a warning such as, "Don't go near any strange dogs!" may evoke nightmarish fear in a sensitive child. A television program or book about a werewolf may become very real to a child who has a strong imagination and has not yet learned to draw the distinction between the real world and the make-believe world. In the child's mind, that strange dog across the street may very well be a werewolf.

In addition to being confused over reality, a child often does not comprehend time and space concepts. Just because a story begins "Long, long ago—" the child does not realize that it is set in the distant past. A child of Deborah's age usually does not have a well-developed sense of time, and such a story, if harrowing, could present an immediate threat.

While waiting in a supermarket line, a child might hear his mother say, "This is going to take *forever!*" This kind of statement could be heard during a 20 minute wait when the child has to use the bathroom. The time, indeed, could seem endless. However, it is a far cry from a trip into another century. The long-ago story, then becomes here and now to the child. The big bad wolf may be brought to mind when a child such as Deborah looks at any wolflike animal. To that child, a strange dog *is* a wolf, and a bad one at that.

Going beyond dogs as such, we began to investigate any hairy or furry objects. In Deborah's case we could find no evidence that she had been frightened by any such thing.

Our inquiries led us nowhere. Then we considered the possibility that Deborah might be jealous of her own dog, having noticed that the family paid more attention to the dog at times than they did to her. At those times she may have needed that attention herself but, out of a sense of loyalty to the dog she loved, she would not betray her need.

It would have been convenient for her to take out her feelings on other dogs which stood for everything her own dog seemed to be taking away from her. Therefore, at the sight of them, she might "act up," making the dog become the mean villain. Her distress signal was the hysterics. It would be translated as, "This dog is mean. You must not like him. Love me instead. I need to be noticed." Her parents would focus their attention upon her and she would get what she wanted and needed.

Actually the cause of Deborah's behavior was brought about, as near as it could be ascertained, by the fact that their German shepherd had been obtained unspayed. As Deborah's parents did not wish the dog to have puppies, they went to great lengths to keep other dogs away. Because Deborah did not understand the mating process, she misunderstood her family's alarm and concern whenever a stray dog appeared.

Deborah saw the stray as a threat to her wonderful new pet,

and sensed that any strange dog would do something terrible to her beloved dog. The dog was spayed eventually, but those first few weeks of real, if unreasonable, fear had their impact upon Deborah. The episode had been almost forgotten by her parents until the psychiatrist's interviews reminded them of it.

Even if the exact reason for Deborah's problem had never been found, treatment could have been given. Many times we cannot find causes for behavior, and yet a child with a problem can be helped by treating the symptoms.

Deborah needed practice in dealing with dogs other than her own to learn that all strange dogs are not harmful. It had to be done through a graduated series of experiences, starting with simple encounters and gradually building up to a point where Deborah could accept strange dogs.

An important aspect of the process was to develop Deborah's independence and self-confidence. She needed to learn to decide for herself, for example, that a particular dog was not a menace. It was essential that she had opportunities to learn from her own experience, all the while receiving assurances of her family's love and acceptance.

Our eventual goal was to have Deborah spend some time alone with a completely strange dog without showing signs of panic.

While there are many ways of introducing a child to a dog, we chose a method considered suitable for a child her age. She loved parties, and one of her favorite games was arranging her dolls and animals around a small table and serving them cookies.

We planned a party for one of her toy dogs. She shared in the plans, selected refreshments and decided who was to be invited. This made her feel important, needed, and secure, because she was to be in the company of those she loved and trusted. The party was a success.

A short time later, another party was planned, the guest of honor this time to be her German shepherd. Over a period of weeks, several such parties were held, at each of which a different dog, known to Deborah, was present. Just one dog at a time was invited.

Finally we manipulated events so that a completely strange dog appeared at a party. Deborah was told at the last minute that the dog who had been invited was unable to attend. The new dog, belonging to one of the teachers at our school, and unknown to any of the children attending the party, was brought into the room. It was a miniature French poodle, well trained and completely obedient. In addition to possessing a lovable personality, the dog knew several captivating tricks.

The dog's owner put it through its paces. The children were delighted at the unexpected show and, when the performance was over, gathered around to pet the poodle. Despite the fact that Deborah had watched with interest during the performance, she hesitated to approach the dog. When she saw the other children petting and feeding the dog, she relaxed a bit. In a little while she joined the group for some ice cream and cake, but still refrained from touching the dog. It was a beginning, though, for she was in the presence of a strange dog and showed no signs of fear.

This was, of course, a very mild and dilute situation for her. She was with friends and with a teacher she knew. Time to observe that the dog was not harmful gave her confidence. It was not the same as being confronted on the street by a strange dog, when she was alone, but it helped her on her way to overcoming her fear.

As time went on, Deborah was able to tolerate other dogs. She became acquainted with many real and make-believe dogs as a result of reading stories about all sorts of pets. Tales in which dogs were fearsome creatures were avoided, while stories about dog-heroes were encouraged, helping her associate dogs with pleasant situations.

COMMENTS

It is obvious that numerous channels can be investigated in searching for explanations of a child's distress signals. I have presented several to give you an idea of some of the ways you can go about looking for clues to behavior. Further, I have treated this chapter differently for a reason. In many previous chapters, actual psychiatric help was not needed. Here I have tried to show you how some psychiatrists work to deduce facts and to investigate sources of problems.

Most children, indeed most people, are afraid of something. Often the fears seem unreasonable to themselves as well as to others, and have no obvious explanation. Even if a distress signal such as fear cannot be explained completely, it can often be treated. In treating Deborah, the psychiatrist employed the reconditioning process. Deborah had developed a certain pattern of behavior that was useful to her by filling her need to get attention and to feel worthwhile. Over a period of time, it became a habit and, as such, was difficult to break. New habits had to be formed to take the place of the old, undesirable ones. To acquire new habits, Deborah needed to be in a receptive frame of mind, free of fear. Sufficient time and patience were needed to accomplish this.

Deborah's fear took on the aspects of a phobia. Phobias arise from hidden sources in the personality and, if extreme, require professional help to overcome. As a result of professional help, Deborah was able to overcome her extreme fear of dogs. While she has retained a healthy respect for the possible dangers of strange dogs, she is able to use her fear in an educated manner, that is, she has developed independent judgment. If she sees a suspicious-looking dog, she avoids it until she learns from a person who knows the animal whether or not it is safe.

Deborah no longer has fits of hysteria, for they have lost their usefulness to her. Her parents have helped her to be more independent. They also gave her the security she needed by convincing her that she has their attention and devotion.

No matter what fear a child may have, you can help by trying to discover and understand its cause. While most children's fears are not as severe or acute as Deborah's, no fear should be treated lightly. Sometimes, fear can be stimulating. Small amounts of it help to keep us alert to danger. When in a dangerous situation, fear enables us to release the energy needed to meet a possible crisis. As long as we keep fear in proportion to the threat we can be reasonably sure that we will be able to handle the situation. But often, as in Deborah's case, a fear can be paralyzing and the child must be helped.

Even if the exact cause of fear is never determined, you can do much to change the child's attitude. You can help the child become independent and self-sufficient by giving him opportunities to cope with various situations over a long period of time, thus helping him to overcome the fear. An important aspect of such a program is the fact that a graduated series of experiences is most readily tolerated.

Time, patience and understanding are essential ingredients of the program. If the child's fear seems too strong for you to handle, it is advisable to seek professional help. This may be obtained from a psychiatrist, a psychologist or a behavioral scientist. Often a family physician or pediatrician will be able to recommend someone capable of handling the situation. In any case, a teacher is wise to remind parents that their full cooperation is needed. Without the family's help and understanding, chances of the child's full recovery are slight, while with full involvement of the family, prospects for full recovery are good.

—————— RECOMMENDED READING

Axelrod, Saul. *Behavior Modification for the Classroom Teacher.* New York: McGraw-Hill Book Co., 1977.

Browning, Robert Mitchell and Donald O. Stover. *Behavior Modification in Child Treatment:* an experimental and clinical approach. Chicago: Aldine-Atherton, 1971.

Goldfried, Marvin R. and Michael Merbaum. *Behavior Change Through Self Control.* New York: Holt, Rinehart & Winston, Inc., 1972.

Marks, Isaac Meyer. *Fears and Phobias.* New York: Academic Press, 1969.

Walker, James Edwin et al. *Behavior Modification: A Practical Approach for Educators.* St. Louis: Mosby, 1976.

chapter 19

Joseph
(A PROBLEM OF PRESSURE)

Viewers of many television commercials frequently see children depicted as the cause of headaches and stomach distress in frantic adults who must deal with their antics. Indeed, an adult who is ulcer-prone may well succumb to an acute attack if exposed to a classroom or household full of noisy, boisterous children.

What many of us do not realize is that children, too, can get stomach ulcers. Joseph was such a child. Outwardly, he was the picture of serenity and as long as the classroom was relatively quiet and he had a well-organized place in which to work, he was happy and symptom-free.

Whenever the other children became noisy or distracted Joseph, he retreated to the book corner or asked to be excused from the room. He did not like games involving competition, and any form of testing disturbed him to the point of nausea or vomiting.

At first, I thought he was an hysterical child who converted his anxieties into physical symptoms. He missed school frequently because of an upset stomach. Before he was referred for psychological testing and counseling, the school nurse suggested a trip to his family physician for a complete checkup.

At that time, various viruses and "bugs" were upsetting the children's digestions. As colds and early childhood diseases often begin with vomiting, the nurse told me that such upsets are not considered serious in isolated episodes. However, Joseph showed symptoms of gastric distress throughout the year, even when the so-called "epidemics of intestinal flu" were not prevalent.

The nurse recalled a previous occasion when a child had been suffering from stomach pains. Because the symptoms were similar to a virus going around at the time, her true condition was almost overlooked. She had a badly inflamed appendix, but only an examination by a doctor, with subsequent laboratory tests, revealed the fact.

We felt that we were not being alarmists, then, by suggesting a trip to the doctor for Joseph. His doctor examined him, and, since no definite cause could be found for the trouble, he prescribed a series of X-rays which revealed the presence of a gastric ulcer.

Joseph was hospitalized for a few days, put on milk and antacid medication, and then released. His mother was instructed to keep him on a bland diet until his ulcer healed. Because ice cream was a favorite with him, the diet was not unpleasant.

He returned to school in a short time, the acute symptoms gone. It was still necessary, however, for him to take medication that decreased the flow of stomach acids. According to his doctor, Joseph's stomach formed too much acid, a condition that may have been partly physical, and partly related to emotional tension.

Effective treatment meant the elimination of stress and anxiety in as many areas of his life as possible. As he spent the greater part of each day in school, this meant that schooltime activities had to be modified to eliminate, or at least to decrease, the amount of stress placed upon him.

To talk to Joseph and tell him not to worry would have been useless. It is next to impossible to tell a person, even the most intelligent and sensible adult, to stop worrying, for it is not a matter of turning off a switch and making the emotional condition disappear. I had to be conservative with Joseph by expecting less from him without giving him the impression that he was falling behind.

Obviously he needed to live up to the great expectations imposed by his parents. They had other children who were scholars and whose academic excellence was a source of pleasure to the family. Joseph was bright but not brilliant, and could not possibly hope to compare with his brothers and sisters.

As an example of his mother's concern over his academic achievement, let me tell you what happened when I changed Joseph from the top level reading group to the low level group.

He needed the change for two reasons. One, he had been absent for a continuous block of time, creating a gap in the skills he needed before going on to other skills. To let him go on would have made him suffer a gap in his learning. He would fall behind, and thus worry more and more. Two, the faster group presented the constant challenge of competition, involved new work, more tension and greater stress. These were things Joseph had to avoid.

I placed him in the low group as a helper, a technique used by many teachers to assure a child that he is not being demoted, and make him feel useful and important. While older children may often see through such a scheme, Joseph, just seven and in second grade, was still quite gullible, enabling the device to work.

It worked, that is, until his mother found out. She came to school in a furious state of mind, charging me with keeping her son from realizing his full potential, annoyed that he was in with the "dumb kids" as she called them.

She was also annoyed that he had missed so much school because of his illness. Not once did she mention how pleased she was that he was recovering from an ulcer attack. As I saw it, the main goal was to raise not a healthy boy, but a scholar in the family tradition.

Eventually, we worked together to create a program designed to help Joseph. Joseph's parents learned to accept him as the child he was. His individual needs and desires were put into focus. He was given modified homework assignments and received just enough work to experience success, but not too much to be overburdened. At one point his father commented, "I guess there's nothing wrong with having *one* average kid in the family."

We tried to make school and home life as stress-free as possible. Joseph was asked to perform only within the limits of his ability. By having a smaller burden, he felt less tension. As he gradually got caught up in his work, he was moved to a higher reading group, but not to the top one.

While some children thrive upon stress and actually need a certain amount of tension to learn, Joseph did not. Of course, he did not understand why he acted the way he did, but he came to accept the fact that things upset him easily and that we were there to help him overcome that sensitivity.

This acceptance was most difficult for him, because he had developed a facade, a show of confidence, which enabled him to appear nonchalant, while inner turmoil burned his stomach. His insides did his worrying for him. His stomach secreted too much acid which created the ulcer. Many medical people feel that some ulcers are in reality "internal weeping."

Since Joseph never cried, I wondered what effect dramatic play would have upon his emotions. If he could become emotionally involved with a character in a play, he might be able to release some of his pent-up emotions. We did several dramatic plays in which Joseph was assigned parts that required the release of tensions such as crying, shouting or becoming angry and attacking another character. Soon he "became" the story-book characters and began to sob realistically, often shedding real tears. I noticed that he seemed able to laugh more spontaneously as a result of the play situations, and he did not shy away from active games as frequently as he formerly had.

One day he pinched his finger in his desk and tried to hold back his reaction. I knew how much it must hurt and how much control he was using to hold back tears. I asked the children to do something special which we reserved for such eventualities. They began to chant, "One, two, three—awwwwww! One, two, three-awwwwww!" over and over again in a silly but sympathetic way, while a few began to giggle. Finally, unable to contain himself any longer, Joseph began to giggle and then to cry. Since silliness can often lead to tears of hysteria, it is impossible to know whether the child involved is laughing or crying. Usually, several join in, and the affected child's emotions are released until the crisis is past.

Because Joseph's fear of failing was so great, I made certain that he would experience some success at least once each day. I made it a point to comment on his performance, the remarks being made just as he left the building so he could carry the positive thought home with him. This gave him a continuing sense of accomplishment. When the school psychologist learned of my efforts in this respect, he recommended that I also encourage him when he entered the classroom, which would assure him that I had confidence in his ability to meet the challenges of the day.

It was planned programming to meet his individual needs, to suit his rate of learning and his ability to grasp new concepts, and to help him accept his limitations. He was never given a task until he was completely ready for it. In that way, he was assured of initial success. Since one success generally leads to others, he began to develop more confidence, which enabled him to proceed to more complex tasks. Yet, contrary to his mother's wishes, he was not given tasks beyond his capabilities and, after a time, she came to understand the plan and began to cooperate fully.

This is the basic concept of the so-called "teaching machines." They have been programmed with material presented in such a way as to assure success at the first try. From there on, the child learns which response is the correct one, and completes one set of responses to the satisfaction of the machine before being allowed to progress to the next step.

If the child is unable to grasp the concept, the work is retraced back to a point where understanding is possible, or presented in another manner, and only then is the child allowed to go on to new material.

This method gives the student a firm basis upon which to build his storehouse of factual or deductive data. If a student begins to fail, he knows he can keep on trying, in other ways perhaps, knowing he will not be punished and that he will ultimately succeed. The reward comes in the feeling of success.

Occasionally the machines are programmed to include complimentary remarks such as "Good work!" or "Keep on, you're almost there!" to encourage the student to continue learning. I feel that many teachers could take a lesson from the machines. These are some advantages of a teaching machine:

1. It evaluates fairly and gives the child the attention he needs all the time.
2. It provides material to meet the individual capabilities of each student.
3. It allows enough time for the student to master the material without becoming impatient or critical.

145

4. It provides reinforcement so that the student is not apt to forget.
5. It makes the goals realistic and within the realm of the student's grasp.
6. It provides encouragement.
7. It captures the student's attention and thus acts as a way of motivating him.

While I am fairly sure that machines will never take the place of human beings as teachers, they have many good aspects. Consequently, they are excellent devices, useful as an aid to the busy teacher. Many commercial "toys" on the market today are actually modifications of these machines.

As a result of the program to help Joseph, he became more relaxed and began to progress. Our program helped him learn without stress, without causing him to break down further. His breakdowns were not visible, in that he did not have tantrums, misbehave or show evidence that most children under stress usually exhibit. He simply allowed his stomach to worry for him, and the symptoms were there.

His biological nature helped create his personality. Joseph will in all probability grow up to be an ulcer-prone individual. Nevertheless, intelligent pacing of his energies and ambitions will do much to counteract the devastating effects of such a personality.

COMMENTS

Most of us associate stomach ulcers with overworked business executives. We think of people who live frantic lives at a hectic pace, picturing individuals who drink too much or smoke excessively or eat the wrong foods. Some of us do not realize that ulcer symptoms can be confused with signs of other disorders. For that reason, I will list the main symptoms of stomach ulcers:

1. Epigastric pain, that is, pain in the upper abdomen.
2. Nausea, or a "sick" feeling.

3. Vomiting, sometimes with a loss of blood if the ulcer is severe or perforating the stomach lining.
4. A gnawing sensation when the stomach is empty. This is the effect of an excess flow of acid on the lining of the empty stomach.
5. Relief of distress upon the intake of food or milk. The relief is temporary and usually the feeling of distress returns after a short interval.

As a teacher or parent, you may recognize these symptoms as characteristic of many childhood conditions. Onset of the common cold or a communicable childhood disease is often accompanied by some of them. Childhood dietary indiscretions, such as eating too many sweets, often cause stomach ache. Young children frequently feel acute distress and pain when they are suffering nothing more than hunger pangs. Cookies and milk will often help a child who feels such pangs.

You can see how a child with an ulcer could very well exhibit merely the same symptoms as a child with no ulcer. Since children *do* fall victim to gastric ulcers, the possibility of its occurrence should not be dismissed just because of the child's tender age. This is particularly true if a child is a natural "worrier" and is placed under stress, or is one who keeps his troubles to himself in a introspective way.

If a child complains of persistent stomach pains and seems outwardly calm, he may be keeping his fears inside and allowing his stomach to take the punishment. In general, many educators feel it is fairly safe to say that a child whose behavior tends to give ulcers to others is not the kind to develop an ulcer himself: He "lets off steam" and releases his emotions.

On the contrary, a child who tends to be withdrawn, who overstrives, who is "nervous" in a quiet way, and who worries is most apt to be the victim of this corrosive disease. It is best to have a doctor examine a child to make sure about his condition. Once the presence of an ulcer is established, you can do much to help such a child in some of the ways mentioned above.

———— RECOMMENDED READING

Bannatyne, Alexander, and Maryl. *How Your Children Can Learn to Live a Rewarding Life: Behavior Modification for Parents and Teachers*. Springfield, Ill.: C.C. Thomas, 1973.
Gray, Jeffrey Alan. *The Psychology of Fear and Stress*. New York: McGraw-Hill Book Co., 1971.
Petrillo, Madeline and Sirgay Sanger. *Emotional Care of Hospitalized Children*. Philadelphia: J.B. Lippincott Co., 1972.
Pinkerton, Philip. *Childhood Disorders—A Psychosomatic Approach*. New York: Columbia University Press, 1975.

Note: Many insurance companies and pharmaceutical companies offer free brochures on a variety of medical topics.

chapter 20

Laura
(A PROBLEM OF REJECTION)

When Laura first entered my second grade classroom, I suspected there was something wrong with her. She took a seat almost too obediently and there she sat quietly and stared into space. When I held up the children's name cards to help introduce them to one another, she failed, or refused, to respond to her own name. Ignoring this, I put her card on the chalkboard tray and made a casual comment about absent children.

Although the children who had been with her in first grade tried to tell me she was present, I changed the subject. As Laura seemed shy, I hoped to direct attention away from her until she gained some confidence.

At recess time, Laura suddenly reached out and grabbed a girl's dress, ripping the seam. Then she stood back, a blank expression on her face, and refused to answer when I asked her what had happened.

On the following day, Laura brought to school a troll doll, soft to the touch, but disturbingly ugly, which she kept with her constantly. Sometimes she held it against her cheek and stroked its hair, her gaze fixed on a point nowhere in the room. It gave me a strange feeling to watch her, for she seemed lost in a world of her own. During the weeks that followed, Laura never laughed, although a fleeting, secret smile often crossed her lips.

Laura had a compulsive need to be clean. Every day she asked to be excused so that she could scrub her hands. When she returned from the lavatory, she brought several wet paper towels which she used to wipe out her desk. Despite the number of assignment papers she did, there were no papers inside her desk. It contained only the barest essentials, always in the same meticulous order.

Laura did her work perfunctorily and without enthusiasm. She did not make many mistakes, partly because she was intelligent, but mostly, I suspected, because she felt a need to be perfect. If I marked a paper to indicate an error, she took great pains to put the paper to rights by erasing every trace of the correction mark. Often she did the entire paper over.

I looked into her family background and found that her biological mother had left home to live with another man. Her father was living with a much younger woman who was expecting a baby. I thought it might prove helpful to discuss new brothers and sisters, as a few other children were going to have additions to their families. Whenever someone mentioned the topic, however, Laura seemed to shut out the conversation. She just sat there, stroking her ugly troll doll and staring moodily into space.

At our Christmas party, Laura did not bring a present for the gift exchange. I knew that she was aware of the situation because the girl who had picked Laura's name brought her gift in advance. In fact, Laura spent a good deal of time fingering the package, trying to see what was inside.

Laura's refusal to bring a gift may have been purposeful on her part. She could have been jealous of the new baby sister that had just arrived at her house and, as a result, may not have wanted to give anything to another child. On the other hand, it may have been because of a lack of interest on the part of her parents, who undoubtedly were busy with the new baby and thus had little time for Laura.

Fortunately, I had a few extra gifts on hand for just such occasions, and slipped one to Laura so she would have something for the girl who had given her a present. Instead of giving away the gift, she insisted on keeping it, along with the one she had received in the exchange. When I tried to explain to her that it was for her partner, she became almost violent. Rather than spoil the party, I gave the other child another gift. The fact that I ignored the incident seemed to incense Laura, who kept telling everyone that she had received two gifts.

I decided to have a conference with Laura's father. He told me that he could do nothing with Laura, that her real mother had left mainly because she hated bothersome kids, and that his bride had all she could do to handle the new baby. Laura, he felt, was in the way. He said he would do anything to avoid her outbursts of temper at home.

When I asked him how he handled discipline problems, he informed me that it was not possible to punish Laura, and that she simply tuned him out when he yelled at her, or yelled back in a fit of temper. He said, "She freaks out. If I didn't know better, I'd think she was taking some drug. The kid's a *weirdo*!"

Such overt rejection from a parent led me to conclude that Laura needed more than the usual amount of attention in the classroom. It had to be attention as a result of her positive behavior, for if she got my attention by "acting up," she would continue to behave in a negative way and her problems might become more serious.

I hoped that she would outgrow her feelings of jealousy for the new baby. Most children will react strongly at first to a new baby in their family, especially if the parents seem to give the baby more attention than they give the older child. I should have said most *normal* children: What I failed to realize was that Laura was far from normal.

During February, Laura was absent for a prolonged period. Many of the children had colds or flu. When Laura returned, I asked her for the required written excuse. She said that her father had not had time to write, but that she had not been ill. She had stayed home to take care of the baby.

When I asked if her parents were ill, she replied that her father had to go to work, and that her stepmother had gone somewhere. Laura had remained at home, feeding, bathing and otherwise caring for the infant until the father could arrange for a baby sitter.

Laura was now quite enthusiastic about the baby. I wondered if she was being truthful; her vivid imagination had invented some extreme fantasies in the past. It seemed unlikely to me that a seven-year-old girl would be put in charge of a young infant, but when I checked with her father, he informed me that Laura was telling the truth.

Laura, indeed, had stayed home to care for her little sister, doing some shopping and simple cooking for herself and her father, and preparing the baby's formula. When the baby had become ill from time to time, Laura's father had appealed to Laura's real mother to help out. The woman had become enraged at the idea of caring for another woman's child. Laura had witnessed the arguments between her father and his first wife.

Despite all this, Laura's personality seemed to change drastically. She came to school eager to talk about the baby. Her face beamed and there was a brightness in her eyes. It was the first real expression I had noted in her. I hoped that she was beginning to accept the baby, and that the responsibility would help her feel important and wanted. She became more interested in her school work, and she even forgot to keep washing her hands.

In one way, I was happy about the change in Laura. Yet, I could not help being concerned about its suddenness. People generally do not change overnight, especially to such an extreme degree.

Laura's happy mood continued for several days, until she was absent once again. When she failed to return after some days, I began to worry that something might be wrong. I did not realize *how* wrong until a case worker returned from calling at Laura's home with the news that Laura had tried to kill the baby by holding a pillow over its face while it slept. Fortunately, her father had returned from work in time to avert disaster.

Laura told the case worker that she had got tired of taking care of the baby. When asked if she thought she had done anything wrong, Laura retreated to her troll doll and hummed under her breath. She smiled the old, secret smile and commented that she liked the doll much better than the baby because it wasn't always throwing up.

Since the father was unable to care for Laura appropriately, it was thought best to have her put into custody of someone who could help her to the best advantage. After many trial situations, Laura was put into a mental institution, where she is currently undergoing psychiatric evaluation and treatment. The treatment consists of psychotherapy and the administration of drugs which are designed to help her become more receptive to the treatment.

She is still young and pliable enough to be helped. While some may consider the damage to her personality irreversible, modern methods of therapy may make recovery possible.

COMMENTS

Signs of unusual behavior in a child are distress signals. Most seven-year-olds are active, energetic, talkative and curious about the world around them. Those who are shy and withdrawn will usually come out of their shells with the right encouragement.

Compulsive behavior, such as hand-washing and desk-cleaning, often express inner conflicts. Sometimes it indicates feeling of repressed guilt, fear or self-pity.

Especially significant is a sudden change in the emotional climate. Laura was dejected, then euphoric, which may have signified that she had determined to solve her problem by eliminating its cause. She tried to get rid of the baby—in essence her problem—in her own way.

Because her parents or guardians seemed to have no consistent code of ethics or moral standards, Laura may have been confused about right and wrong. You might say she was forced into taking the action she took, for it was the only way she knew how to solve the problem. Nothing mattered to her except to get rid of the object of her father's affections. Once the unwanted baby was eliminated, she thought she would have her father's attention and love again.

Laura had symptoms of a rejected child. She was deprived of the love and attention she needed. Because she did not receive affection from her parents, she was incapable of bestowing affection upon her baby sister. Her self-confidence was corroded, her self-esteem was undermined, and she felt helpless, insecure and frustrated.

She finally reached a point where she was unable to cope with reality. We do not know if she was aware of the implications of her act toward the baby. Her world was so mixed up and her despair so great that she was probably incapable of rational thought.

Rejected children have little hope of recovery if the rejection continues. They usually suffer personality damage to some degree. The signals of distress may be different in individual cases. Bed-wetting, nailbiting, feeding problems, stuttering, antisocial behavior and aggression are just a few manifestations of the effects of rejection.

Rejection is a general term. You may ask, "What would a parent have to do to be rejecting his child?" If a parent answers "Yes" to any of the following questions, his child may be in danger of rejection:

1. Do you ignore the child and turn your interests elsewhere?
2. Do you criticize him constantly and sometimes unfairly?
3. Do you punish him for minor misdeeds by spanking or by verbal threats?
4. Do you nag at him constantly?
5. Do you neglect his welfare?
6. Do you compare him unfavorably to others?
7. Do you fail to listen to his troubles, or to acknowledge his accomplishments?
8. Do you give him anything he wants just to "get him out of the way"?
9. Do you supervise his every action in an overprotective manner so that he cannot develop self-confidence?
10. Do you give him your love or attention only when he performs the way you wish?

As you can see, an affirmative answer to any of the above questions may indicate a parent's lack of interest in a child. The lack of interest may not be intentional; the parents may be busy people, or they may think they are doing the right thing because they, themselves, were treated that way and they "turned out all right." Nevertheless, each child is a unique individual with special needs, and the adults in his life must do what is best for him.

It is not often that a teacher in an ordinary classroom will be confronted by a child as deeply troubled as Laura. Although hers was an unusual case, it *did* occur in an average classroom situation.

It reminds us to be ever watchful for extremes of behavior in children. It is advisable that such behavior be treated immediately. This does not mean that a teacher or parent should play pseudo-psychologist. Children within the normal limits of behavior can, and will, often respond well to attention from a teacher or parent who directs them in a helpful manner. Some cases, such as Laura's, benefit from the help of specialists.

Teachers can refer such students to the school psychologist for testing and discreet counseling. They can direct worried parents to take the child to a qualified person, such as a psychiatrist, psychologist or clergyman. Many cities have "hot lines" and will list telephone numbers to be called for directions when such troubles occur. Check your telephone directory for the local number to call a clinic, children's hospital or doctor.

Fortunately, young children respond well to treatment, for they are usually pliable enough to endure a great deal before permanent harm is done. Nevertheless, quick action on your part will make the process of rehabilitation easier for everyone concerned.

—————— RECOMMENDED READING

Adams, Paul L. *Obsessive Children—A Sociopsychiatric Study*. New York: Brunner/Mazel, 1973.

Bryson, Carolyn Q. *Early Childhood Psychoses*. Rockville, Me.: National Institute of Mental Health, 1971.

Clarizio, Harvey F. *Behavior Disorders in School-aged Children*. Scranton, Pa.: Chandler Publication Co., 1970.

Kanner, Leo. *Childhood Psychosis*. New York: J. Wiley & Sons, Inc., 1973.

Reinert, Henry R. *Children in Conflict*. St. Louis: C.V. Mosby, 1976.

Szurek, Stanislaus A. *Clinical Studies in Childhood Psychoses*. New York: Brunner/Mazel, 1973.

chapter 21

Philip
(A PROBLEM OF HYPERACTIVITY)

When Philip entered my second grade classroom, he was accompanied by a folder filled with reports about his disruptive behavior in first grade. Although such terms as *hyperkinetic, overactive, minimal brain dysfunction,* and *inattentive* repeated themselves with regularity, I did not have to open his folder to know that something was wrong with Philip. He simply could not sit still for more than a few seconds at a time.

While I attempted to take attendance, Philip hopped from desk to desk in a frenzy of motion. He squealed and grunted, clapped his hands, grabbed other children's crayons and bumped against their arms as they tried to color pictures.

Until his arrival, the children had been quietly absorbed in coloring some pictures. They were asked to match their crayons with a color chart on the wall to keep them occupied while I completed a few clerical tasks. Teachers are reluctant to assign "busy work" such as this, but it is inevitable at times. The completed pictures would help me determine who knew colors, who handled crayons well, who could follow directions, who could read color words, and who was colorblind.

It was obvious that I would not discover any of these things about Philip, for he persisted in moving around. He broke each crayon into little bits, and tossed the bits about the room. Some of the children complained about being hit by chunks of crayon. I could see why his first grade teacher had considered him disruptive.

Instead of coloring his picture, he folded the paper into a crude airplane and hurled it through the air. Then he ran after it, again and again, while I presented him with other papers, hoping that he would eventually settle down. He seemed to be aware that I disapproved of the paper tossing, so he switched to scissors and began cutting the paper into small pieces. When he had collected a pile of scraps on his desk, he commenced to blow them off onto the floor.

If his large leg muscles were not being used in running around, his smaller hand muscles were in motion. He folded, tore, cut or tossed papers. Even the muscles of his mouth were in constant movement as he blew scraps from his desk. It was obvious that he did not do this out of "naughtiness," for when I asked him to clean up the fragments from the floor, he complied. It was in a rather unusual manner, however. He did not bend down and pick up the papers, but rather removed his shoe and sock from one foot and grasped the papers with his curled toes. Then he hopped on the other foot as far as the wastebasket, put his foot into the wastebasket and released the paper from his toes.

I was fascinated by his obvious coordination. What he did took skill, yet his records showed that he was unable to learn reading and writing. As the days passed, it became more and more obvious to me that Philip was not acting the way he did in order to gain attention. When he noticed the children watching him, he usually returned to his desk for a few moments. It was as though he could not help himself.

Time after time I thought he was ready to settle down, as a few minutes passed without any extreme movements. Then he moved his body in another way, sometimes opening and closing his desk in rhythmic motions, all the while rocking his body back and forth to an inner tune with a definite beat.

During the weeks that followed, Philip became more of a problem. The children were learning to write their names on second grade paper, but Philip continued to mutilate the paper. Occasionally he rolled it into balls and tossed them into the wastebasket, missing his aim more than hitting the target. It was futile to scold him, for he merely ceased the activity for which he was reprimanded and changed to a substitute action.

He was unable to do the usual classroom assignments. The children, by that time, were capable of sitting at their desks long enough to read a story or write some numbers. Their studies were intermixed with short intervals of action to change the pace and give their muscles a chance to stretch and relax. Anyone dealing with young children knows the importance of changing tempo. It prevents boredom, and gives the children the physical activity so necessary to their growing bodies.

Most of my group adapted themselves to the routine nicely. The more active children made unnecessary trips to the pencil sharpener or the drinking fountain, but I considered that normal movement. The *constant* movement of Philip was a sign that something was wrong.

I decided to confer with Philip's parents in the hope that they would be able to tell me more than I had learned from his record cards.

Philip's mother was disturbed by his "souped-up" behavior. "He's a human windmill," she said. "He doesn't come to rest for a minute, just like a pesty fly, buzzing around. Even when he's watching TV, he's crawling all over the floor. You should see his bed after he's been asleep—a disaster area!"

I asked her how long he had been this way.

"He was born with his mainspring wound too tight," she answered. "He's faster than the other kids—learned to walk earlier. I sure wish he could read."

Then I asked her what reading might interest him. A parent can often give a teacher insight into a child's interests, and make it possible for the teacher to offer reading material that will catch the child's attention for a sustained period.

Her answer was evasive. She said, "I believe he could read if he could sit still long enough to open a book. I've tried everything. I've even tried a special diet for him. Someone told me that food additives cause a lot of this restlessness in kids. I took him off ice cream and junk food, you know, stuff loaded with preservatives, for a whole month."

As I had heard about a theory similar to the one she mentioned, I asked her what she thought of the results.

"Not too much," she said. "Some people claim it works like a charm. Maybe I don't understand enough about food additives. Some day I'll learn more and try it again. I'll try anything!"

We agreed that "some day" might prove too late to help Philip. It was important to do something for him now.

The first step was to have him interviewed by a psychologist. She found that Philip could read, write and compute numbers. To my surprise, his raw test score was 50 percent, which meant that he was about average in his academic work, and not below the level as everyone had believed.

Philip was also tested by a doctor, a neurologist and a psychiatrist. He proved to be a perceptive child, to my surprise remembering the names of everyone who examined him, and recalling many of the technical phrases they had used.

If he was able to remember such things, then why was he unable to do school work? Why had other teachers felt that he might have minimal brain dysfunction?

Because MBD (minimal brain dysfunction) had been mentioned in earlier reports from another school, Philip was given a test to measure brain waves; his patterns were found to be just slightly abnormal.

To make it possible for Philip to settle down in the classroom as soon as possible, a drug was prescribed for him. The psychiatrist believed that a small dosage of *Ritalin* might help. Ritalin is actually a stimulant to the central nervous system. In some individuals, it has a calming effect by stimulating the area which "calms down" the patient.

As his teacher, I was asked to watch him closely for the first two weeks after he began taking Ritalin The only side effect he suffered was a mild dizziness. He actually seemed to enjoy the sensation, talking about how "good" he felt. Many young children like the sensation of vertigo, often rotating their bodies around and around until they fall down. Some experts compare the feeling to that of being intoxicated.

The doctor decided that this dizziness was not serious enough for him to stop the medication. No skin rash developed, nor did any other adverse reactions occur. After the second week, though, I noticed that Philip seemed preoccupied and lethargic. I brought this to the attention of the doctor, who decreased the dosage, and eventually the right dosage was determined.

Philip began sitting still for longer periods. He joined the reading groups early in the day. Toward late in the afternoon, however, when the effects of Ritalin wore off somewhat, he became restless once more. At those times I let him take something from the activity table. He liked to pound clay and mess with fingerpaint.

Before taking medication, Philip had pounded and pummeled

159

the clay. Now he began to roll it into a "dough" with a rolling pin, and to cut the dough into "cookies" with cookie cutters. Instead of tossing the clay cookies into the air or out of the window, he arranged them on a tray and showed them to me.

When he first began doing this, he would rush to my side and thrust the tray toward me for immediate attention, often shoving or pushing aside other children who were there first. Entering or leaving the room, he ran instead of walking, often tripping or falling down. We learned that this "awkwardness" was not caused by "brain damage" or "nervous disorder," but rather by the fact that he had never been trained to act properly. Once he was able to settle down and learn to do some things in a certain way, he became more receptive to learning many other things.

COMMENTS

Philip's problem was not as serious as everyone had at first believed.

Eventually he settled down to a relatively slower pace, and was able to pay attention to one subject for longer intervals. After he became interested in a subject, he began to show some success in it, and each small success was rewarded. There were times, of course, when he became restless and overactive. Then the dosage of his medication was increased.

Medication alone was not responsible for the change in Philip's behavior. Once a week, he visited a psychiatrist for counseling. His parents participated fully in the treatment procedures. The psychiatrist made it clear that it is essential for the family to share in the treament and to understand what is happening.

Some parents are reluctant to have their child evaluated by a psychiatrist, mainly because it means being interviewed, too. They are afraid they may be found to have problems of their own, which they may not care to admit. Nevertheless, the discovery of a parental problem often helps to understand a child's problem. The psychiatrist can best help a troubled child by knowing the child's total home situation. A teacher is wise to advise parents not to feel defensive about seeing a psychiatrist, for if it will help the child, it is worth the soul-seaching involved.

One of the most frequent complaints made by parents today is that their child is overactive. Ordinary activity should not be confused with *hyperkinesis,* which refers to exaggerated motor activity and excessive restlessness, symptoms found in both physical and psychological disorders. Philip's case is an example of a mild aspect of the condition.

Whatever the cause, physical or psychological, the fact remains that many hyperactive children are unmanageable in school or at home, and need help.

You may wish to know more about some of the symptoms a child with minimal brain dysfunction exhibits. The term *Minimal Brain Dysfunction* (MBD) generally implies certain behavioral or learning disabilities which may be mild or severe, and which are associated with deviations of function of the central nervous system. Some manifestations of the condition are:

1. Perceptional disturbances in which a child cannot "put together" what he sees or hears. He has trouble learning to talk, read, sing or dress himself.
2. Faulty spatial perception. A child may judge distances or directions improperly. He might have a tendency to trip, fall, bump into things or otherwise appear to be "clumsy."
3. A child may persist in one act, such as repeating the same tune or chant over and over again for weeks at a time.
4. A child may have a short attention span. This is generally caused by his inability to "tune out" unimportant details. He is thus easily distracted.
5. A child may be unable to form associations, such as associating sounds with symbols in the reading process.
6. A child may be unable to make generalizations or see similarities and differences.
7. In addition to the above perceptual and conceptual dis-

turbances the child may exhibit behavior disturbances such as:

acting like a much younger child;

lacking self-control and crying or laughing too readily;

being hyperactive or impulsive;

being overtalkative or restless;

behaving in a destructive or aggressive manner;

acting in a discouraged or frustrated way;

assigning "live" characteristics to inanimate objects.

Most "normal" children will occasionally exhibit any or all of these symptoms briefly. Persistence of the symptoms suggests a problem.

The range of symptoms is generally so wide that each child must be treated on an individual basis. The help should be specific for the child. To give you an example of the broad range of treatment, here are some activities which have been used with success:

1. The child is encouraged to play with lifelike animal toys. He can feel, touch and examine their forms and learn about their physical qualities.
2. The child is given colored beads to handle. This helps him to recognize form and substance.
3. The child is given nesting boxes to help show him relationships in size and depth.
4. The child is encouraged to play with toys that help his motor coordination. These may be wind-up toys, scissors, nuts, bolts or screws.
5. The child's hand-to-eye coordination can be improved by allowing him to work with hammer-and-nail sets.
6. Fingerpainting, tracing letters or numbers with sandpaper models, using tracing paper, and similar activities help the child to move his body in correct ways.
7. Finger plays encourage the child to engage in group activities. Most book stores have volumes on various finger plays. The most common one taught by parents for many generations has been, "This little piggy went to market."

8. Counting activities often prove helpful. The child must learn a one-to-one relationship. He can be encouraged to do this in the schoolroom by counting children and getting a chair for each one.

In my own personal experience, I have found a most helpful way to teach a child relationships and I have suggested it to many grateful parents. It works well with most children, and even extremely hyperactive children have derived some benefits from it. I allow the child to help with dinner preparations. By setting a dinner table, the child gets valuable practice in counting people and places. He sets the places to accommodate the correct number of guests, *including himself,* an important aspect of the procedure.

At first, he uses place mats which helps him to locate each place. As he puts plates and silverware upon each mat, he gains practice in determining left and right, top and bottom, inside and outside.

A simple act such as removing pickles from a jar with a fork is a valuable experience. Be sure to loosen the cap before asking the child to open the jar. He will have to rotate it the right way before it comes off. He will also have to hold the jar upright to prevent the juice from spilling out. Do not be disturbed if he spills pickle juice on the counter top or floor, just ask him to wipe it up. This will engage his large muscles, help him to see cause-effect relationships, and encourage him to *try.*

In spearing a pickle on a fork, he gains practice in aiming for an object and grasping it with a tool, he learns depth concepts, and he has an opportunity to learn about measurement. The jar is tall while the pickle dish is flat. The dish may not hold all of the pickles that were contained in the jar.

After he has mastered the pickles, let him try arranging olives in a similar way. Unlike flat pickle slices, olives are round and have a tendency to roll. This will help the child observe qualities in form and function. If the olives are stuffed with pimentoes, ask the child to remove the pimentoes. A toothpick is good means by which to do this. Wooden toothpicks are to be preferred, for they often break during such operations, and the child must therefore learn to hold them in a certain way at the correct angle to prevent breakage.

163

You may be confronted by a messy dish of pierced olives and broken pimento bits, and wonder who will eat them. I am sure some of your guests will cooperate by complimenting the child's efforts. If not, pretend that they are pleased, for the child's sake. He will feel that he has done something useful for someone else.

If you are finicky, as I am, be sure the child washes his hands carefully before he helps. By all means, show him the way to use soap and water. Many of us assume that children know how to do simple things such as washing their hands. This is not necessarily so. Demonstrate each step and then allow the child to wash his hands. Have some attractive, sweet-smelling soap. Be sure the water is not too hot or too cold. If necessary, let the child stand on a stool so he can see what he is doing and feel comfortable in the process. Do not wash his hands for him, as he will never learn to handle soap and water that way.

However, do not overdo the hand-washing by insisting that the child do it too often. He may come to regard it as an unpleasant chore and try to avoid it. We sometimes have a tendency to go to extremes with cleanliness. Keep in mind that, as someone once said, an ideal home is clean enough to be healthy, but messy enough to be happy.

Many children who are hyperactive are restrained from the abovementioned type of activities because they might create havoc. Yet, the only way they can learn to accomplish tasks is by doing them. We must make an effort to give the child every opportunity to try.

I have found that once a child begins to experience success instead of failure, he feels more confident. This, in turn, often prompts him to try other endeavors. If we channel the child's activities into useful outlets, we may help him overcome much of his problem.

———— RECOMMENDED READING

Archuleta, Alyce J. *The Hyperactive Child*. (A Selected Bibliography for Parents and Educators). San Diego: Current Bibliography Series, 1974.

Conrad, Peter. *Identifying Hyperactive Children*. Lexington, Mass. Lexington Books, 1976.

Renshaw, Domeena C. *The Hyperactive Child*. Chicago: Nelson-Hall, 1974.

Schrag, Peter and Diane Divoky. *The Myth of the Hyperactive Child*. New York: Pantheon Books, 1975.

Smith, Lendon H. *Improving Your Child's Behavior Chemistry*. Englewood Cliffs, N.J.: Prentice-Hall, 1976.

Afterword

In reading through the preceding stories, you may have recognized some problems which have affected children you know. Undoubtedly, many teachers and parents could add cases from their own experience.

I have written about those in which I was most involved. As you have seen, the children's problems were detected through their distress signals. I trust that you have gained insight into the nature of those various signals and may be able to recognize them readily in the future.

Once a problem is found to exist, you may consider several solutions. The specific problem may have elements similar to those in several different cases I have cited. Thus, you may wish to glean a few hints from each case and adapt them to meet an individual need.

In many cases, the teachers and parents were able to handle the problem satisfactorily by working at it together. Other times, the help of a psychologist was required. In a few instances, psychiatric assistance was necessary.

In reading these stories, you see, for example, how *pressures* of one type or another can affect a child. Tommy was unable to cope with school. He was afraid of failure and ridicule. He was exposed to parental and peer pressures, from which he escaped through psychosomatic means. To help Tommy, realistic goals were set. He was provided with tasks that could be accomplished, and his successes were praised. Thus, he developed self-confidence.

Sarah was a victim of *stress*. Her case helps us to understand some of the physical and emotional aspects of speech disorders and allied conditions. She overcame her stuttering when she realized that the adults in her life were interested in her and trying to help her. We encouraged communication through mutual understanding.

Another manifestation of *stress* occurred in Holly's case. She was a supersensitive child who literally worried herself sick. Her physical symptoms developed when she was under emotional stress. Holly's case helps us to see how a child can become willing to try new tasks without fear of failure. We learn some ways to handle tension and worry. By knowing in advance what was to be expected of her, Holly developed confidence in herself.

We learn some ways to modify behavior and establish positive attitudes. We also learn the importance of encouragement rather than criticism. If a child is given an opportunity to do as many things as possible with success, that child's self-confidence will become stronger.

Joseph, too, was under pressure. His story disproves the fallacy that only adults get stomach ulcers. As we learn more about Joseph, we see how ulcers can be related to stress and pressures, both physical and psychological. We learn the symptoms to watch for, and become aware of the importance of modifying the life style in order to prevent a recurrence of the trouble. Several ways to decrease stress are suggested.

Some of the children were *handicapped* in one way or another. Andy's handicap was partly physical and partly psychological. He never listened. As we read about Andy, we see some methods of recognizing various handicaps. Diagnostic tests are suggested. We see how a handicap can be overcome or how a child can adapt to it. Once we gained Andy's attention, we kept it by adding interest and variety to his activities.

Sometimes it is not the child, but the parent, who has a handicap which affects the child. Melissa was the child of deaf-mute parents. Her home life was quite different from her school situation. She had special problems in both places. Melissa had to overcome the attitudes of outsiders. She had to learn to live a "normal" life despite the double standards imposed upon her. Her behavior was directed toward positive goals. We learn some ways to help her conform, and also how to prevent embarrassment for her.

Gary was too big for his age. His *abnormality* was *temporary*. By reading Gary's story, we gain some insight into the problem of oversized and overweight children. We see how self-conscious Gary was, and how peer criticism affected him.

We learn some ways to overcome the emotional reactions resulting from such a problem. Hypergrowth of the body is presented as both an asset and a liability, depending upon how it is treated.

Janet had a *permanent abnormality*. She was too small for her age, with no hope of ever growing to normal size. Although her physical and emotional problems were difficult to deal with, yet she adapted to her situation. We see how she was directed toward realistic goals, and how common sense helped develop her confidence and self-reliance.

The stories of two children help us to understand the problem of confused sexual roles. Both Michael and Frances had a problem of *deviance*. Michael exhibited signs of homosexuality. Its causes are explored. We learn how a child's interests and attitudes may be directed toward socially accepted roles. The changing attitudes of today's society are brought into focus. Suggestions for adjustmens are offered, with emphasis upon when they should or should not be made.

Frances, who acted and dressed like a boy to gain her mother's attention, was encouraged to emulate womanly behavior and to comprehend acceptable sexual roles. We are warned against making generalizations about behavior that may seem to indicate sexual deviance.

Amy was a sexually mature child. Her problem was of *physical precocity*. Her unusually early maturation created physical and emotional problems. Ways to prevent such a child from feeling different are enumerated. We are shown how to avoid feelings of guilt, and to treat sexual matters with the right mixture of objectivity and warmth.

Fear was Deborah's problem. She had an unreasoanble and extreme fear of strange dogs that amounted to a phobia. The basic causes of fear in most children are explained. We become acquainted with types of fears and their manifestations. We learn how fears develop. We discover how to overcome fears by gradual behavior-modification techniques. Numerous specific suggestions are made.

Carl also lived in fear. His problem was one of *psychological trauma*. He went through a marked behavior change as a result of an unpleasant experience. We learn that parental prejudices may have detrimental effects upon children. Methods are given to help change attitudes and modify behavior without causing further trauma.

Tim had a problem of *emotional release*. He witnessed his father's death. We become aware of various methods to explain death to children. We learn how mourning can be therapy for bereaved children. We are warned of the danger of excluding certain children from the circle of mourners.

Facing Death is the subject of Darlene's story. However, it was her own death, and involved a problem of philosophy. Should a child with a terminal illness be informed of impending death? Can such a child sense a poor prognosis without being told? We are made aware of the reactions of afflicted children, their parents and teachers. We learn ways to explain the condition to' the child, and ways to help the child enjoy life.

Brian's problem was one of *perspective*. In his story, we go into the dangers of overrating ability that is based on the child's social background. What effects do high expectations have upon the child's self-image? We learn the importance of being direct and yet discreet in dealing with an exceptional child.

Morality is the subject of Karen's story. Karen exemplifies the child who steals, lies or cheats. We learn the causes of such behavior, and how faulty patterns develop. We learn ways to teach a child right from wrong, and the effects of open confrontation and punishment.

Robert thought money could buy anything. His problem involved *judgment*. His values were confused. What incentives motivate affluent children? What rewards exist for children "who have everything"? Do they have everything? If not, what are their special needs? How can these needs be met? These, and other questions, are answered in Robert's story.

One of the most frequent problems confronting today's children is *hyperactivity*. Philip was a hyperkinetic child. In his story, we learn some of the physical reasons for his behavior. A psychiatrist explains how tranquilizers or central nervous system stimulants may be used in conjunction with behavior-modification therapy. We learn the importance of emotional and physical release in overactive children.

The *rejected* child is discussed in two stories. John was abandoned by his parents. We learn how rejected children often react. We also learn how we may win a child's confidence and strengthen his self-esteem. Suggestions are made to help create a feeling of security by making the child feel loved and wanted.

Unlike John, Laura's rejection caused her to retreat into herself. She had a serious mental disturbance. We learn how it could have developed and its possible causes. What are the dangers of ignoring threats of violence? Where can we seek professional help in serious psychological problems? Laura's story contains some of the answers.

You will notice that certain basic elements occur again and again in many of the stories. Yet, each problem is as unique as the child himself. The similarities exist because all of the children are human beings. As such, they have basic human needs and desires. When those needs are not met, the child suffers. How he reacts depends upon his nature and his development.

Now that you have become acquainted with many forms of distress signals, I hope that you may find it easier to understand a child's behavior. If you apply some of the methods that were used with success in the cases included in this book, you may be able to offer help to a troubled child.

In dealing with my problem children advice was given to me by professionals in many fields. As a result, I was able to take part in helping many children. My reason for writing this book is to pass on the knowledge and insights I have gained to others who have responsibility for children. If just one child is helped as a result of this book, I will feel that I have been a good teacher.

RECOMMENDED READING

Baker, Katherine Read. *Ideas that Work with Young Children*. Washington: National Association for the Education of Young Children, 1972.

Bakwin, Harry and Ruth Morris Bakwin. *Behavior Disorders in Children*. Philadelphia: Saunders & Co., 1972.

Douglas, James. *The Home and the School*. London: Macgibbon and Kee, 1964.

Dreikers, Rudolf. *Psychology in the Classroom*. New York: Harper & Row, 1968.

Frank, Irving. *Psychosomatic Ailments in Childhood and Adolescence*. Springfield, Ill.: C.C. Thomas, 1967.

Goldenson, Robert M. *The Encyclopedia of Human Behavior*. Garden City, N.Y.: Doubleday & Co., 1970.

Klein, Roger D. *Behavior Modification in Educational Settings*, Springfield, Ill.: C.C. Thomas, 1973.

Kliman, Gilbert. *Psychological Emergencies of Childhood*. New York: Grune & Stratton, 1968.

Krumboltz, John D. *Changing Children's Behavior*. Englewood Cliffs, N.J.: Prentice-Hall, 1972.

Lerner, Janet W. *Children with Learning Disabilities*. Boston: Houghton Mifflin, 1971.

MacMillan, Donald L. *Behavior Modification in Education*. New York: The Macmillan Co., 1973.

Palmer, James O. *The Psychological Assessment of Children*.New York: Wiley, 1970.

Poteet, James A. *Behavior Modification: A Practical Guide for Teachers*. Minneapolis: Burgess Publishing Co., 1973.

Rogovin, Ann. *Learning by Doing*. Johnstown, Pa.: Mafex, Associated, 1971.

Sheen, Fulton J. *Children and Parents*. New York: Simon and Shuster, 1970.

Vargas, Julie S. *Behavioral Psychology for Teachers*.New York: Harper & Row, 1977.

Index